PAUL ROBESON

The Life and Times
of a Free Black Man

VIRGINIA HAMILTON

*For Etta Belle and Kenneth J. Hamilton,
and all who came before.*

A LAUREL-LEAF BOOK
Published by
Dell Publishing Co., Inc.
1 Dag Hammarskjold Plaza
New York, New York 10017

Laurel-Leaf ® TM 766734, Dell Publishing Co., Inc.

ISBN: 0-440-96806-2

Reprinted by arrangement with Harper & Row, Publishers, Inc.
Printed in the United States of America

First Laurel-Leaf printing—June 1979
Second Laurel-Leaf printing—August 1979

PAUL ROBESON was an athlete, scholar, singer, and actor. He believed in equality for himself and for all people, and he wasn't afraid to say so. When Robeson was born in 1898, hardly any opportunities were available for black people in America. While still in school, he determined to make something of himself— and he did. He won a scholarship to college, became a lawyer, and later turned to the theater. By the late 1920's he had become well-known as an actor and concert artist. At the height of his popularity in the 1930's and 1940's, he was loved and respected throughout the world.

A few years later, his own country rejected him because of his political ideas, and his career was broken. Even so, millions of people continued to support and cherish what he stood for and today new generations of Americans are rediscovering Robeson, the humanist and political activist.

VIRGINIA HAMILTON was born in Yellow Springs, Ohio. After many years in New York and other cities, she returned to Yellow Springs, where she lives with her husband and children. Ms. Hamilton is the author of the National Book Award and Newbery Medal Winner, *M.C. Higgins, the Great*, and the ALA Notables: *Zeely, The House of Dies Drear*, and *The Planet of Junior Brown* (also a Newbery Honor Book). They are all available in Laurel-Leaf editions.

THE LAUREL-LEAF LIBRARY brings together under a single imprint outstanding works of fiction and nonfiction particularly suitable for young readers, both in and out of the classroom. The series is under the editorship of Charles F. Reasoner, Professor of Elementary Education, New York University.

Grateful acknowledgment is made for permission to reprint from the following:

"Ballad for Americans." Words by John Latouche, music by Earl Robinson. Copyright 1940, renewed 1967, Robbins Music Corporation, New York, New York, & Fred Fisher Music Co., Inc.

"The Ballad of the Spanish Civil Guard" from *New Masses, An Anthology of the Rebel Thirties*. Edited with a Prologue by Joseph North. Copyright © 1969 by International Publishers Co., Inc.

Here I Stand by Paul Robeson. Copyright © 1958 by Othello Associates; Beacon edition, Boston, 1971.

"Joe Hill" from *Songs of Work and Protest* by Edith Fowkes and Joe Glazer. Copyright © 1973 by Dover Publications, New York.

"Ode to Paul Robeson" by Pablo Neruda. Translated by Jill Booty.

"Ol' Man River" from the musical production *Showboat*. Music by Jerome Kern, lyrics by Oscar Hammerstein II. Copyright 1927 by T.B. Harms Company, copyright renewed 1955.

Paul Robeson: Negro by Eslanda Goode Robeson, Harper & Row, Publishers, Inc. 1930.

"Tribute to Roosevelt" by Carl Sandburg, read by Mr. Sandburg at the meeting of the Independent Citizens' Committee of the Arts, Sciences and Professions. Used by permission of the Carl Sandburg Family Trust.

Appreciation is given to biographer Marie Seton for pertinent material for which her book *Paul Robeson* (Dennis Dobson, London) is the sole source.

Contents

The Knowledge

I'm running home. I am quite young, I am happy, for I've won a prize for having read the most books during the year. The prize is a good-sized, shiny book with the colorful cover parading three yellow ducks. It was my first award and more glorious for being what it was—a new book, which was never easy to come by in my childhood. Ever after, I have been an ardent reader, not only of books but of most anything—old match covers, catalogs, whatever falls into my hands.

My family always encouraged my reading and, when I began to write at the age of nine or ten, did not think to discourage that, either. Perhaps a writer writes for young people especially because her own youth recurs in the mind more often than any other segment of her life. My childhood was particularly fine if we allow for the fact that I had no concept of dollar poverty. We had land and plenty to eat. That my parents struggled for both was beyond the realm of my understanding.

My childhood was rural and completely absorbing. And I don't remember, as a child, ever wanting to be anything else. It was a time when we children were expected to be seen and not heard, to have spotless manners, to speak properly when the preacher came by the house, to entertain ourselves, to go to bed early and be out of the house in summer to play by nine o'clock. In short, we—I and the children of my relatives—were on our own from sunup to sundown. Sometimes, when we felt like it, we helped with chores, such as feeding chickens or pulling morning glories entwined around the corn. But mostly, we played. No one expected me to come directly home after school, wash dishes, clean the room I shared with my sisters or get in the way. I never did. My mother demanded that I stay on the honor role, that I go to Sunday School, be home by dark.

Otherwise, I was free to roam to neighboring farms owned by my mother's people, the Perrys, where I had cousins and aunts and uncles always glad to see me. Eventually, I ranged some distance from home to the other side of town and the glen (Glen Helen, a thousand-acre wildlife preserve of forest, hill and dale and old Indian trails now owned by Antioch College). In the glen, I discovered deer, the sweet and yellow freshwater springs, an immense, condemned pavillion once a grand hotel and marvelous old vines strong enough to swing on.

At the age of nine or ten, I became a business-woman, having discovered that the mustard and dan-delion greens that my mother was so fond of were also loved by all of her churchgoing friends who did not live on farms. So I picked the greens by the basket in the morning and had sold two or three baskets by early afternoon. I soon expanded my marketable pro-duce to include strawberries, blackberries and rasp-berries in season. I took on a business rival as a part-ner: my cousin Marlene, who, barefoot the same as me, would accompany me down the hot highways as we made our daily business rounds. The quarters of profit we immediately sank into the local movie house, where three times a week we sat through the delightful and terrifying horror of old and new Wolf-man and Frankenstein films. Always, we remembered too late that afterwards we would have to run more than a half mile out of town down a pitch-black road to get home. Nevertheless, our business flourished—as did our fright—until we outgrew both.

Such occurrences of my childhood—the atmosphere, if not the incidents—find their way into my books. So it happens that I write first for myself for the sheer joy of evoking these memories, through which a certain knowledge of the past is brought into being and made to live again.

Biographies such as this one of Paul Robeson also grow from my understanding of the past and childhood, and from a very unique process of learning which went on in black families of the time and period of my youth. Education, with a capital E, took place in public school, with all of its aspiration to honor rolls and its agony of shameful failure. But *the Knowledge*—knowledge about *us*—came from home and usually from our fathers, just as it did in the life of Paul Robeson. Now, *home* included our church, the African Methodist Episcopal congregation, which could, on occasion, cause the mind of a child to explode with knowledge. I remember one fateful day when a visiting black man stood before the pulpit and recited all of the parts of a play called *Green Pastures*. I had never before witnessed such a feat of memory or portrayal, and promptly became the gentleman's shadow until he left town, no doubt to entertain other congregations.

In the public schools in the 1940's, we black children were taught little that might suggest that our people had contributed any lasting virtue to the American experience. We were taught with rather too much sympathy that our ancestors had been slaves. This fact often threw our teacher into a kind of tearful reverie, after which she would say, "Now we will sing 'Old Black Joe.'"

What we were to learn of the pride and of the dignity of our people came from home. It was an intensely private knowledge which I don't remember discussing with any of my white classmates. And if they had knowledge of black accomplishment they never imparted it to me.

My father, Kenneth James Hamilton, had *the Knowledge* in our household, and on still summer evenings in the country, he endeavored to pass it on to his children. I, being the youngest, most often sat at his side on the porch to listen. In the background of this learning process were the melodies gently wafting forth from his mandolin, which he played softly as he spoke. The rink-a-tink sound of the mandolin always gives the past for me a special harmony.

When Kenneth Hamilton had answered all of my questions as best he could, about the summer stars, and death, and nightfall and its purpose, he would begin with *the Knowledge*. He had particular reverence for Dr. W.E.B. Du Bois, the black scholar. But there were others, such as singers Florence Mills and Blind Lemon Jefferson, whom he said he knew. A few were white, having become part of *the Knowledge* through some contribution to our people, whether for good or bad. Jack London, the writer, was one of these. My father knew him when he was a young boy, not yet a famous writer but an older youth, something of a tough against whom my father played baseball. London was quick with his fists, so my father said, and sharp with his tongue against blacks and Jews.

Others of the blacks were men such as Joe Louis, the boxer, called the Brown Bomber, and of course Paul Robeson.

Like many Americans, my father must have heard Paul Robeson sing over the radio at one time or another. He must have read about Robeson's extraordinary feats of daring and skill on the football fields of Rutgers. But however he came by his knowledge of Mr. Robeson, he gave it his special rendering. So that by the time I heard of this great man, he embodied much of my father's hopes and dreams for his own children. Not fame, particularly, but attitude.

"I imagine," Kenneth Hamilton would begin, "that Mr. Paul Robeson woke up one morning to find there was more to the day than playing football. I know I did [Kenneth Hamilton played football for Iowa State]. I imagine he looked around him. He saw that plenty of his people already were preachers; there were enough morticians to reach from here to kingdom come. I imagine Mr. Robeson decided then and there he would be what there never had been before. And he was."

I don't recall Kenneth Hamilton ever saying what it was Paul Robeson became besides a football star. But surely he was referring to Robeson's powerful singing voice. Yet what came through clearly to me at the time was this: If one were to become anything, it would have to be not only the best but wholly original, a new idea. This concept sank deep into my consciousness. Imperceptibly, I grew up yearning for the unusual, seeking something unique in myself. I longed not just to write, but to newly write and like no one else. Kenneth Hamilton wanted no less for his youngest child.

Like no one else, he had been no less himself. Graduating from Iowa State Business College in the early 1890's when it was an achievement when a black man completed high school, he began his search for employment.

One day, the banker for whom his mother worked as a cook asked that young Kenneth be sent around to the bank, where there was a suitable job for him. Kenneth Hamilton hurried over to the bank, absolutely amazed at this sudden stroke of luck. Dressed in starched collar and grey business suit, he wondered what would he become—a teller to start, passing out crisp, new money with proper manners and a smile? Or maybe he would sit behind a desk, assuring his favorite customer that the second mortgage would be no problem, no problem at all.

Kenneth Hamilton passed under the marble facade into the bank and was promptly handed a mop and a bucket. He threw both the length of the establishment and turned on his heel, never to return. Soon after, he left his home as well, to become a restless wanderer ranging the length and breadth of the North American continent, seeking but never quite finding that for which he searched.

Perhaps he should have accepted that first mop and

bucket, but I'm rather glad his imagination wouldn't permit him. For now I have the pleasure of remembering him as a man who would not allow mind or body to be limited by another's reality. I could have wanted no less for a father.

Today, it seems quite natural that I should come to write about the life and times of Paul Robeson, a black man of utmost character and accomplishment, of whom, unfortunately, a generation of Americans has never heard. For he was more than one man, more than a symbol for blacks like my father whose dreams had been thwarted. Through his art and the spoken word, Robeson had an amazing ability to project to the world his profound understanding for his people. For black America, he embodied an age-old Spirit of Survival, beginning with the battle of slave revolts and continuing on through the protest battles of modern times. Not even when cotton was king was that Spirit ever quelled; for half a century, Paul Robeson was that Spirit for an entire race.

Today, *the Knowledge* of Kenneth Hamilton, my father, has come full circle. It gives me pleasure that from his special rendering of Mr. Robeson some thirty years ago has come my own.

Virginia Hamilton

VIRGINIA HAMILTON
Yellow Springs, Ohio

1

Paul Leroy Robeson had the good fortune to have been born into a large and close-knit black family. His roots went deep in the American dream of equality. For his ancestors had survived the turmoil of the Civil War to grasp the promise of freedom at the war's aftermath. He grew strong, surrounded by the warmth of Robeson love and pride of a family determined never to be re-enslaved. He had wonderful uncles who were big, powerful-looking men, just like his father. They had bold, masculine names, such as Benjamin, Uncle Reeve and Uncle John. The names of his female cousins, Carraway and Chance, brought to mind spice and flavor freely combined with luck.

Long before Paul Robeson was born, his own father, the Reverend William Drew Robeson, was the undisputed leader of the Robeson people and the beloved patriarch of the family church.

Paul didn't just love his father, but loved him "like no one in all the world." Reverend William Drew Robeson was a man of medium height, with broad shoulders and great dignity of bearing. He had the finest speaking and singing voice Paul had ever heard. The boy loved walking at his father's side and holding tightly to his hand as the Reverend Robeson conversed with and comforted his parishioners.

Paul's grandfather on his father's side of the family was a slave born a piece of property on a plantation close to Raleigh, North Carolina. The grandfather had been given the Christian name of Benjamin by the whites who owned him. His black ancestors who were brought forcibly from Africa had names either unknown or hard to pronounce by white people. They too were given Christian names. And so it was that Paul's grandfather became known merely as Benjamin, black slave owned by whites named Roberson. Benjamin married Sabra, also a slave of the Robersons, and from this marriage was born Paul's father, William Drew, on July 27, 1845. When he was fifteen years old, William Drew ran away from slavery. And slightly changing the "Roberson" surname of his former owner, he became William Drew *Robeson*.

At the age of sixteen in 1861, William Drew Robeson joined the Union Army when Civil War broke out between the North and the South over the issue of slavery. And when the war ended in 1865, William Drew came north as did thousands of black people leaving the South. His brothers Benjamin and John came also. His nieces Carraway and Chance came, following William to Princeton, New Jersey, the home of one of America's oldest and most valued universities.

By this time, William Drew had learned to read and write. After an elementary education, he thought about going to college. He couldn't go to Princeton University, however, for it was an all-white school with a student body dominated by wealthy southern white youths. No black students were admitted. This situation at Princeton clearly revealed to William Drew that although black people were no longer slaves, they weren't exactly free and equal, either, not even in the North.

Back in the South, southern states defeated in the Civil War were reorganized. New laws were passed making blacks free, and equal to whites. But legal freedom was not a guarantee that black people would have equal rights. Soon, the blacks were to embody a new southern dominance and become the servants upon whose backs the South would rise again.

William Drew Robeson attended Lincoln University, a black school situated near Philadelphia, Penn-

sylvania. He studied to be a minister so that he might
serve his people spiritually. And while at Lincoln, he
met Maria Luisa Bustill, a very pretty woman and a
Philadelphia schoolteacher. She had light brown skin,
straight, dark hair and a dramatic combination of
English, Indian and African features. Maria spoke the
"thee" and "thy" form of address used by the religious
Society of Friends, or Quakers.

Her great-great-grandfather, Cyrus Bustill, had
English Quaker ancestry as well as Indian and black.
Quaker settlers from England had founded Burlington, New Jersey, in 1677, and Cyrus was born a slave
in Burlington in 1732. Much later, Cyrus bought his
own freedom and became a baker in Philadelphia,
where he was also a leading member of the city's free
black community. During the Revolutionary War, Cyrus baked bread for the hungry armies of George
Washington not twenty miles from Philadelphia at
Valley Forge, Pennsylvania. Other leading blacks
along with Cyrus founded the Free African Society in
1787, the first brotherhood and mutual aid society organized by blacks in America.

Other Bustills in this period were teachers and sea-
men. During the Civil War, one was a "conductor" on
the Underground Railroad, and one a painter for
whom it is said Abraham Lincoln posed. Still another
one, also a painter, was Robert Bustill, who studied in
London at the National Gallery of Fine Arts.

Maria Luisa Bustill married the dark-skinned William Drew Robeson when she was twenty-six years
old and he was thirty-one, on July 11, 1878. And with
their marriage, the Quaker, black and Indian stock of
the Bustills combined with the Bantu African stock of
the Robesons, making for strong and individualistic
offspring. Of the six children born to them over the
next twenty years, five lived to adulthood. William
Drew, Jr., the oldest, became a medical doctor practicing in Washington, D.C. Reeve, called Reed, moved
to Detroit and became a businessman. Benjamin,

known as Ben, became a minister like his father. Their only daughter, Marion, was a schoolteacher in Philadelphia as had been her mother before her. Paul Leroy, the youngest and strongest of the Robeson children, was born on April 9, 1898.

Paul Robeson's birth occurred at the time of a new age in America. The North, which had been victorious in the Civil War, now was no longer held back industrially or financially by the slaveholding South and the West. Urban and northern America swiftly developed into an area rich in energy and imagination. Individual men who operated businesses were bold and ruthless; they exploited equally the natural and human resources of a whole country.

In the years between 1888 and 1901, the United States dominated the western hemisphere and attempted to subjugate darker people inside America as well as outside. When the U.S. went to war with Spain and won, Spanish Cuba became the means for obtaining dominion over all of the Caribbean. Moreover, America took possession of the Philippine Islands, Puerto Rico and Guam, as well as Cuba and all former possessions of Spain, and acquired Hawaii. Northern business interests united with southern leaders against black Americans in a concerted effort to drive blacks out of political parties. Thus, southern blacks could be exploited as a voteless servant class and a source of cheap labor.

Prejudice, ostracism and violence had the effect of thwarting black advancement at every turn. Black leaders such as William Scarborough, classical-Greek scholar and linguist, spoke out angrily at the cruelty shown to blacks:

> They are shot down if they testify against white men; they meet the same fate if they refuse to do so. If they attempt to assert their civil and political rights in any manly way they are mobbed, butchered, and killed.[1]

* * *

Nevertheless, black people continued to struggle for freedom in the face of immense difficulty, as did the Robeson family.

As a young child, Paul Leroy Robeson knew all of the warmth and love of an ambitious, hardworking family determined to better itself. He grew, chubby, happy, in the large, comfortable parsonage to which his father had first brought his bride. His mother wrote as many fine sermons as his father, and also helped to educate the family. Maria Robeson was not a Presbyterian like her husband, but she was able to instill into her family the gentle, peace-loving virtue of her Quaker beginning. For Paul and his brothers and sister, her understanding devotion formed the security that was their daily homelife.

As a minister, Paul's father had achieved the highest position of attainment then possible for blacks in America. And as pastor of the Witherspoon Street Presbyterian Church, Reverend Robeson was held in esteem by his black community and duly tolerated with a somewhat grudging regard by the larger white society. Those who lived well and had money in Princeton were white people, and those who worked for them were black.

"The pastor," as Paul was to write, "was a sort of bridge between the Have-nots and the Haves, and he served his flock in many worldly ways—seeking work for the jobless, money for the needy, mercy from the Law."[2]

So it was that the sympathetic, friendly Reverend Robeson served his community, until tragedy struck his household in the winter of 1904.

Paul's mother, increasingly bothered by cataracts on her eyes, caught her clothes on fire at the parlor stove. His brother Ben was at home and tried desperately to help his mother beat out the flames from her floor-length skirts. Neighbors, hearing terrible screams, burst in to help. But it had all happened too quickly, right before Ben's horrified eyes. Even though a doctor was called, Maria Robeson died in a few hours from severe burns.

Although quite young, Paul attended the funeral and saw his mother lying in her coffin. There were relatives who came quickly to comfort him. But seeing her there was no less a shock for him.

"I remember her lying in her coffin, and the funeral, and the relatives who came," he wrote years later, "but it must be that the pain and shock of her death blotted out all other personal recollections."[3]

Paul probably suffered most from the sudden death of his mother. He was not quite six years old when she died. But in the extended Robeson family, there was no sudden departure of love in his life. As always, there were loving aunts and uncles to protect and comfort him. There were his brothers and his sister to lean on. There was his wise and wonderful father, who remained for Paul larger than life.

Of more immediate effect on Paul's life was that his father soon lost his post as minister of the Witherspoon Street Presbyterian Church through some church dispute. Almost at once, Reverend Robeson had no income. He had no savings and for a few months was forced to find work hauling ashes. Finally, he became a coachman, with the white southern college students as his rich clientele.

Reverend Robeson struggled hard to feed and clothe and educate his children. William Robeson, Jr., the eldest son, was soon out of the house and away at college to begin his career. Marion and Reeve lived with relatives. Later, Reverend Robeson was able to send his son Ben to Biddle University, and Marion to Scotia Seminary, both in North Carolina. For a while, Reeve stayed in Princeton, but he soon got into trouble with the law. Working as a coachman to southern white students as did his father, he refused to take their racial slurs. Reeve fought many a young bigot with his fists. Reluctantly, Reverend Robeson asked him to leave. For fighting back against powerful whites was begging disaster, and Reverend Robeson feared Reeve would become an unfortunate example for young Paul.

Often as not, Paul woke and slept comfortably with the children of his relatives. Cornbread was regularly his dinner, breakfast and lunch, along with nourishing mustard greens or dandelion greens. Happily, Paul passed in and out of aunts', cousins' and friends' households. He attended segregated black schools in Princeton and lived totally within a black world. No blacks were allowed to attend the Princeton high school. Paul's brother Bill had been forced to go to Trenton eleven miles away in order to attend high school.

Generally, Paul took part in the social life of black children, playing football and baseball and all manner of other games of childhood.

"There were the vacant lots for ball games," he was to write years later, "and the wonderful moments when Bill, vacationing from college [Lincoln University] where he played on the team, would teach me how to play football. He was my first coach, and over and over again on a weed-grown lot he would put me through the paces—how to tackle a man so he stayed tackled, how to run with the ball."[4]

In the homes of his friends and relatives, Paul learned the loyalties of race and clan. Ever after, he would be grateful to aunts, uncles and cousins not long freed from tobacco and cotton fields of North Carolina.

Three years after the death of his wife and the loss of his ministry, Reverend Robeson moved from Princeton to Westfield, New Jersey, where he started life over again. He found work in a grocery store owned by a sympathetic woman called Miss Fannie. Nine-year-old Paul and his brother Ben joined their father in Westfield. There, they lived in the attic close under the roof above Miss Fannie's grocery store. They used the shack attached to the rear of the store as their washroom and kitchen.

In Westfield, Paul was able to attend integrated

schools. There were so few blacks in the town that the white community had little reason to fear them or need to segregate them. Each morning before he went to school, Paul carried grocery deliveries for Miss Fannie.

Reverend Robeson soon returned to his religious calling; not as a Presbyterian minister, however, because of the conflict he had with the church in Princeton. He formed a group of African Methodists, with whom he built the Downing Street African Methodist Episcopal (A.M.E.) Church. The time Paul and his father and Ben spent in Westfield lasted only until the Downing Street Church was established. But for the whole period, Paul was well aware that his father wanted more than anything for him to be happy. He was the youngest child and therefore his father's greatest worry. Reverend Robeson was getting on in years. Now in his sixties, he grew anxious for his young son, and worried about how well Paul would get on in school. However, Paul tried his best to get good grades.

Once a month, he received his report card from school. Reverend Robeson went over the report, with Paul good-naturedly peering over his shoulder. When Paul's card was rather good, Reverend Robeson was pleased. But when the report card showed all A's, he was warm and open in his praise for Paul.

Once, Paul brought home six A's instead of the usual seven.

"What's the idea of the B?" Reverend Robeson asked him.

"But Pop," Paul said, "I'm ahead of everyone else in class. My teachers thought these grades were fine."[5]

His father smiled thinly, it seemed to Paul. Then he assured his son that they would have to spend more time on Latin, the subject in which Paul had received a B.

Next month, Paul proudly showed his father the report card on which he'd received all A's. He had learned quickly that perfection was what his father expected of him.

Often now, however, loneliness would overcome him as he walked home from school. He knew he mustn't trouble his father about it. But down that street where he lived and played with neighboring children, he wondered about their mothers, so quick to laugh and to smile at him. Suddenly, he knew how deeply he missed having a mother of his own, whose pride and love would touch his heart.

These natural feelings of a motherless boy he was wise enough to keep to himself. He and his father soon moved on to Somerville, where there was a black school run by a black educator. Right away, Paul attended Mr. James L. Jamison's school. Ben was now attending Biddle University. Marion was at Scotia Seminary and William was at Lincoln. Reverend Robeson became the pastor of the St. Thomas A.M.E. Zion Church. And he would spend the remainder of his life at Somerville, New Jersey.

Paul was twelve years old in 1910. He was tall and athletic, with an open friendliness that made him a favorite of the students. He was the biggest fellow in Mr. Jamison's school and the smartest in his class. One year later, he entered Somerville High School, one of two black children attending the school. He joined the school glee club and discovered that he had unusual ability in music.

Yet, musical ability did nothing to rid him of some amount of self-consciousness, which he had developed over the years. Later, he would write about this time:

> I was always remembering that I must not do this or that, or I must not hit a boy back because I was colored. . . . In my classes I had to stay up late to prove that Negroes could also measure up in their studies.

He also wrote about something he remembered from living in Princeton:

Something strange, perhaps, and not easy to describe. I early became conscious—I don't quite know how—of a special feeling of the Negro community for me. I was no different from the other kids of the neighborhood—playing our games of Follow the Leader and Run Sheep Run, saying "yes ma'am" and never sassing our elders, fearing to cross the nearby cemetery because of the "ghosts," coming reluctant and new-scrubbed to Sunday school. And yet, like my father, the people claimed to see something special about me. Whatever it was, and no one really said, they felt I was fated for great things to come.[6]

Paul took courses in Greek, Latin, history, literature and philosophy, chemistry and physics. If his grades were not the highest, he had to answer to his father. However, Paul was very bright and his grades were fine. His teachers seemed to encourage him especially. He joined the drama club and his English teacher gave him the title role in Shakespeare's *Othello*. His music teacher instructed him in the proper use of his voice. Only the high school principal seemed to dislike Paul. It was because of this man that Paul learned he had an explosive temper like his brother Reeve.

He played football, which the principal opposed. He was soloist with the glee club and again the principal tried to keep him from this honor. Angrily, he told Reverend Robeson that he would fight the principal if the principal so much as touched him. Reverend Robeson had told the teachers that they might discipline the high-spirited Paul whenever they thought it necessary.

Always somewhat shy, Paul slowly learned to control his temper by withdrawing within himself. Inside himself was a fierce pride and a dream to be always the best in everything. Deep within him there lived a certain yet lonesome security in the memory of his long-lost mother. Sudden aloofness or withdrawal would become a trait of his personality throughout his life.

In the field of sports, Paul was able to transform his shyness into the power of physical movement. Brilliant in athletics throughout his high-school career, he was aggressive and equipped with fine coordination.

During the summer, he worked at menial jobs in a restaurant at Narragansett, Rhode Island. His brother Ben also worked there, as a waiter. Paul had done such work since the age of twelve, mopping floors and peeling potatoes from five in the morning until late in the evening. Having to work made him different from the others in his school, who were white and came from comfortable homes. But working gave him the opportunity to learn about the outside world. He soon discovered how strong was his sense of purpose.

In his last year in high school, he found out there was to be a four-year scholarship to Rutgers College for anyone who could score highest on a competitive examination. Paul had not taken the preliminary examination which the other students had passed the year before. They would be tested on work covering only their senior year. If Paul took the test he would have to be examined on four years of study. But even though he would be at a disadvantage, he was sure he could win over the other students.

Such confidence seemed like the fantasy-wish of a downtrodden youth. But Paul knew himself better than anyone. He knew his own mind and the power of it. Furthermore, Reverend Robeson encouraged him to take the examination. And Paul won the contest.

In the spring of 1915, he graduated from high school as an honor student at the age of seventeen. Besides his singing ability and athletic prowess, he had become the finest debater in his school. That summer, he joined a statewide oratorical contest, which he lost to a white girl who placed first and to a fellow black who placed second. Still, he had received his scholarship to attend Rutgers, and he was happy.

Paul knew he might be even happier attending the black school Lincoln University. Both his father and his brother William had gone there; Lincoln would welcome another Robeson with open arms while white Rutgers might not be so accepting of him. But he had won the Rutgers scholarship over all other competitors and against all odds. This was one of the most important facts of his life up to now.

Alone and cut off from other blacks, he might feel self-conscious at Rutgers. The surrounding world might try to deny him equality. But at last he decided to go to Rutgers. For beyond a doubt, inside himself, he knew he was not inferior.

In the fall of 1915, Paul entered Rutgers; the New Jersey institution was then famous for its football team. He continued the classical studies which he had started in high school. He also became the captain of the Rutgers debating society and won numerous prizes for his superb oratory. Coached by his father in refined public speaking, Paul learned to express his own opinions with powerful ease.

Football in 1915 was more a brutal game of speed and physical endurance than it was a scientific sport. Rutgers had a fine team; and as a freshman, Paul tried out for the second-string "scrubs," as the reserves were called. Coach Foster Sanford was frantically preparing his team of thirty players for Rutgers's big game against Princeton. And any young man who had the vaguest notion about football could try out and might possibly even play. Coach Sanford wanted on his team that huge black fellow named Paul Robeson, and Robeson had shown interest in joining. But half of the white players told Sanford that they wouldn't play if the "black boy" was on the team and in the game against Princeton. They made sure he wouldn't make it by putting him out of action. And years later, Paul would tell about the other football players who were white:

> Well—they didn't want a Negro on their team. . . .
> One boy slugged me in the face and smashed
> my nose. . . . When I was down, flat on my
> back, another boy got me with his knees, just

came over and fell on me. He managed to dislocate my right shoulder.[1]

Paul was in bed for ten days. He had plenty of time to think, and now he wasn't sure how much more abuse he could take. Maybe he should just leave Rutgers and go on to Lincoln, where he knew he would be wanted and needed.

"Well, I didn't know," he said. "My brother came to see me, and he said, 'Kid, I know what it is. I went through it at Pennsylvania. If you want to quit school go ahead, but I wouldn't like to think, and our father wouldn't like to think, that our family had a quitter in it.' "[2]

Paul may have been just a seventeen-year-old student but he wasn't a quitter. He stayed at Rutgers, letting his wounds heal and taking abuse day after day from white "scrubs." But one time, he let loose his temper:

"A boy came over and stepped, hard, on my hand. . . . The bones held, but his cleats took every single one of the fingernails off my right hand. That's when I knew rage!"[2]

Not stopping a second because of his injury, he caught up with the ball carrier in the next play and heaved the boy over his head: "I was going to smash him so hard to the ground that I'd break him right in two, and I could have done it. But just then the coach yelled . . . 'Robey, you're on the varsity!' "[2]

After that incident, Paul was treated with respect, and he went on to play football for Rutgers for four years. As a fine athlete, he was as accepted in college as any black man then could hope to be. He became a discus thrower in field games, and finally a four-letter man, playing baseball and center on the basketball team. He was a member of Walter Camp's All-American team in 1917 and 1918. And already, sportswriters paid tribute to his athletic ability:

* * *

He rode on the wings of the frigid breezes; a grim, silent, and compelling figure. . . . It was Robeson, a veritable Othello of battle.[3a]

A dark cloud. . . . Robeson, the giant Negro.[3b]

Paul became the mainstay of the Rutgers football team, although he was never quite its hero. In 1918, he was even pulled out of the lineup when Rutgers played the southern college Washington and Lee University. The college objected to playing football against a "negro" so Paul was withdrawn from the team for that game. And yet, he was given the affectionate nickname of "Robey" by his white classmates, who were proud and open in their admiration for him.

Paul was a member of the Rutgers student council and in his junior year was elected to Phi Beta Kappa, America's national honor fraternity. Moreover, he had won the spring contest for extemporaneous speaking each year, using his sonorous, deep voice to perfect tone and understatement. But he never sang with the Rutgers glee club because after each glee club performance there would be a college dance. And he knew he would be stepping dangerously hard on the color line if he attended these dances. Reluctantly, he forced himself to be careful, contenting himself with his other considerable accomplishments.

During the whole of his college career, Paul never forgot about his father in Somerville, New Jersey. He made a trip home usually every week to let Reverend Robeson know what he was doing at school. After hearing how his father was, Paul liked to hear about all of his friends and relatives. Always, his father cautioned him to remember that his studies came first, before everything else. Reverend Robeson eagerly turned out to see Paul play football and to cheer along with his son's growing number of fans. He became a regular on the front bench of the cheering section and a booster for the whole of the football team.

At the end of Paul's junior year, on May 17, 1918, Reverend Robeson died at the age of seventy-three.

Paul was heartbroken, without a home to go to any longer and without the one closest to him who had guided his life for so long. Paul's struggle to live became even more difficult. Yet he was able to graduate from Rutgers in 1919 by working the menial jobs in Rhode Island as he had each summer of his college career.

But even in the face of his personal loss, his ability and achievement had steadily mounted, and by the end of his senior year seemed almost unbelievable. He was a debating champion. He gave the commencement speech at his graduation and also won thirteen varsity letters in four sports. He won election to the Cap and Skull Honor Society with three other men who represented above all others the traditional ideals of Rutgers: personality, athletic achievement and scholarship.

Paul had a right to be proud. And carefully now, he took stock of his two hundred pounds of tough, physical strength. Within himself, his blackness seemed coiled, waiting to spring forth in all of its power. Having moved far from the life of his dead father, who had been a slave, he had grown up with the belief that he was destined for greatness. He knew he had to be a credit to his race, and this he never doubted or objected to. Always, he carried with him the memory and spirit of his father. At odd moments throughout his life, he often said to himself, "How'm I doin', Pop?"

However, Paul had no idea what destiny awaited him nor what life work he would pursue. In college, he had taken the liberal arts curriculum which included courses in political science and in constitutional and Roman law. His senior paper was written about the Fourteenth Amendment and the American Constitution. Still, the question of his future career left him anxious as well as eager.

After graduation, Paul moved to Harlem, the black community nestled on the Harlem River in New York City. During World War I, black people left the South to escape racial violence and moved to northern cities, where there was a wartime demand for workers. Between 1916 and 1919, black populations doubled in the cities. And while the war boom lasted, new city blacks held an uneasy truce with northern whites, who felt the blacks were intruding into white territories and taking white jobs.

After the war ended, clashes between the races were frequent and violent whenever blacks attempted to move beyond their ghetto districts into all-white bordering areas. Living overcrowded in often miserable tenements, the blacks wanted only a decent life. But whites saw their expansion as an attack on themselves, their way of life. They fought hard to keep blacks out. When unsuccessful, they moved away.

By 1919, Harlem was well established as a black area in New York City. With a population ever increasing in size, it had a life reflecting the atmosphere and varied traditions of its black people. There were lovely churches, fine, beautiful homes. There were doctors, dentists and recent graduates from the best American universities. Every kind of business operated there and every sort of person lived there, from worker to professional. So that when Paul Robeson moved to Harlem, he felt as if he had turned a corner of a familiar Princeton street and come back home.

Paul's interest in law increased, and early in 1920 he entered Columbia University Law School, working at odd jobs in order to pay his fees. He was already well known in Harlem as a great sports figure and a man brilliant at academics as well. Everyone wanted to shake hands with the towering man who had made them so proud of him on the playing fields of Rutgers.

At Columbia, Paul played basketball and coached choral groups, with which he often sang. Twice, he played professional football and earned a staggering $1000 for each game. But in the 1920's, paid athletes were considered tainted or criminal and Paul wouldn't consider making his living as a professional player.

The First World War had ended two years earlier.

Now, money was easier to come by, at least for the white population; and people couldn't wait to spend and to have fun. Dance halls around New York's Broadway were always full and frantic. Plays and movies experienced a popularity as never before. Jim Europe, a black bandleader, had taken the new American music, jazz, to France with him during the war as the leader of the 369th Colored Infantry Band. He brought jazz back with him after the war, and people could now dance to his swinging orchestra at the Winter Garden.

Whites with money came quickly uptown to Harlem to hear the new jazz and to find new ways to spend their money. They "discovered" Harlem, and the black man came into style.

This golden age in Harlem became known as the Negro or Harlem Renaissance. Black poets, writers, painters and actors flourished as never before and brought a special vitality to American arts and letters.

Robeson, like so many others of his people, strode through the streets of Harlem feeling his own strength and the might of his race surge forth. He continued to study law at Columbia, but he watched the world of Harlem and waited—for what, he wasn't sure. He hoped his intuition would suggest to him the direction his life would take; for a career at law never seemed quite right to him.

By ordinary chance, he became an actor. The Harlem branch of the Y.W.C.A. asked Paul to play the lead in a drama entitled *Simon the Cyrenian*. The drama was one of *Three Plays for a Negro Theatre* by the white lyric poet Ridgely Torrence. Simon was said to have been a black African who had carried Christ's cross to Calvary. *Simon the Cyrenian* was considered a turning point in the depiction of blacks in American theater. For this drama no longer showed blacks as stereotypes to be laughed at, but as real people of human depth.

Paul didn't waste a moment deciding whether he wanted the part. He was delighted and accepted at once. He made his debut as an actor and as Simon in 1920. In the opening-night audience was Ridgely Torrence himself. Others present were members of the Provincetown Players (later known as the Provincetown Playhouse), an experimental theater in Greenwich Village. The Playhouse's principal playwright was Eugene O'Neill, who refused to write the usual popular plays about the upper-class life of the rich. Instead, he created works about life on oil tankers or in the dark, dank tenements of Harlem. After Paul acted the role of Simon, the founders of the Provincetown Playhouse gave him warm congratulations.

Paul accepted the applause for his performance and his warm welcome into the professional world of acting with the poised detachment that would become the mark of his public style. Privately, he always knew he would continue to be outstanding, for his father had taught him that in order to remain simply equal, black people would have to perform better than whites.

> From an early age [Paul was to write] I had come to accept and follow a certain protective tactic of Negro life in America, and I did not fully break with the pattern until many years later. Even while demonstrating that he is really an equal (and, strangely, the proof must be *superior* performance!) the Negro must never appear to be challenging white superiority. Climb up if you can—but don't act "uppity." Always show that you are *grateful*. . . . Above all, *do nothing to give them cause to fear you, for* then the oppressing hand, which might at times ease up a little, will surely become a fist to knock you down again![4]

Paul viewed success as the necessary outcome of a committed life. Yet he did not want whites to fear him or make difficulties for him. So he held himself aloof and looked upon his first acting experience as something of a milestone on the road to success.

After his performance as Simon, he went home as though nothing too extraordinary had taken place. Early the next morning, he was back in law school, still waiting for his intuition to lead him to his life's career. He came to believe that his opportunity to become an actor was a strange sort of luck, an excellent odd job that had very little to do with the outcome of his life.

Although he didn't take his acting debut seriously, the founders of the Provincetown Playhouse certainly did. They had worked with all sorts of actors, from beginners, hardly able to walk across the stage without tripping over themselves, to seasoned veterans. They realized that the unusual intuitive sense that Paul Robeson depended on in his role as Simon could be the wellspring of his talent as an actor.

The Playhouse now offered Paul the lead in *The Emperor Jones*, a new play by Eugene O'Neill. In the play, an ordinary black man, Brutus Jones, becomes Emperor of an island of blacks, who eventually rise up to destroy him. With great anger, Paul scornfully refused the lead. He found the play disgusting, with blacks traipsing through an island jungle like savages. Moreover, acting still meant to him a way to survive while he attended law school. He knew he was headed somewhere, but acting didn't seem to be the place. So it was that his career as an actor was thwarted by him alone in its beginning.

A year later, he met Eslanda Cardozo Goode, a student in the Chemistry Department at Columbia University Teachers' College. Eslanda, known by her friends as Essie, was a fiery young woman of considerable intelligence and talent.

One of Essie's ancestors was Francis Cardozo, a black slave owned and later freed by the white Cardozos of South Carolina. Francis Cardozo had been sent by the white Cardozos to Glasgow University in Scotland to be educated. When Francis returned to

America, he founded Avery Institute, the first school for blacks in South Carolina. After the Civil War, Francis became South Carolina's Secretary of State.

The strong-willed Essie made a great impression on Paul. She was unusually critical and outspoken about black-white relations for the times in which she lived, and was violently angered by the inferior positions forced upon blacks. Paul was not any less resentful inwardly. But he had proved himself as a scholar and as an athlete; he seemed to have talent as an actor. Although he wasn't yet satisfied, he showed an inner confidence which caused him to appear much more relaxed and easygoing than the energetic Essie.

Their friendship grew and deepened; in the autumn of 1921, they were married in Rye, New York. They found an apartment in Harlem; Essie was graduated from Columbia Teachers' College and became the first black to obtain a job as an analytical chemist in the Surgery and Pathology Department of Columbia Presbyterian Medical Center. Before this, blacks held only menial jobs in hospitals. They were not admitted to nursing schools, nor did white medical schools train black doctors. And black patients were not admitted to white hospitals. So when Essie obtained her position at Columbia Presbyterian, it was an unusual breakthrough for all blacks. She was justly proud of her success, and so was Paul. He continued with law school. Occasionally, he played professional football. He coached teams and continued singing.

Then, rather suddenly in 1922, Paul was offered a leading role in the play *Taboo*, written by Mary Hoyt Wyborg. Paul accepted the part and played opposite the famous English actress Margaret Wycherly. Yet apparently his performance wasn't spectacular, for the leading New York critic, Alexander Woollcott, was sure Robeson should give up acting for *any* other career. Years later, however, Woollcott became a great admirer of Paul on and off the stage. He invited Paul to his home and the two became good friends. In his

autobiography, *While Rome Burns,* Woollcott was to
write about Paul:

> Paul Robeson strikes me as having been made out
> of the original stuff of the world. . . . He is a
> fresh act, a fresh gesture, a fresh effort of crea-
> tion. I am proud of belonging to his race. For, of
> course, we both are members of the one some-
> times fulsomely described as human. . . .[5]

Paul went to London with *Taboo,* which had been
retitled *Voodoo,* in the summer of 1922, and then on
tour with it throughout the English counties. He
would never forget his first impression of England.
He found the people kind and friendly, and he did not
witness any of the prejudice he had left behind in
America.

After his tour, Paul returned home to America and
to his law studies at Columbia. In the spring of 1923,
he graduated from Columbia Law School. Essie expected him to search at once for a job with a law
firm, for hadn't he struggled all these years for just
such a career? But Paul hesitated. He didn't know
quite how to begin to practice law. Was he to join up
with the powerful Democratic Tammany-Hall politicians who controlled New York City? They had offered him a job, a good job, too. But he was afraid he
would have to do what they told him to do, and so he
refused the offer.

Paul waited—and for what, he wasn't certain.
Months went slowly by. Essie watched as others of
Paul's classmates found good jobs. Occasionally, he
found work singing in Harlem's famed Cotton Club,
where black actress Florence Mills was the star. But
purely by chance, he did one day find steady work. A
trustee of Rutgers University had a rich law firm
downtown. He knew Paul's career, and he offered
him a job with the law firm, which handled many important law cases. Paul gladly accepted and was soon
writing law briefs on several of the firm's cases.

Other young members of the law firm never looked kindly on having the "black giant" among them. Sensing trouble, the Rutgers trustee suggested that Paul open a branch of the firm in Harlem. But Paul felt there was little law work available in Harlem. The important black businesses of Harlem all had white attorneys. He could not see himself sweating over minor divorce cases, and finally refused the offer. A few weeks later, one of the firm's white secretaries declined to take dictation from him. Hurt and disillusioned, Paul marched out of the law office, never to return.

But luck always seemed to be close to Paul, whether he recognized it for what it was or not. Something turned up in the form of the Provincetown Players, who had not forgotten his performance several years before as Simon the Cyrenian. Early in 1924, Director James Light and his associate, Kenneth Macgowan, offered Paul the lead in two plays by Eugene O'Neill. The plays were *All God's Chillun Got Wings* and a revival of *The Emperor Jones*, which Paul had turned down in 1920. This time, he accepted both offers.

"I needed money," Paul said. "The [$]75 a week which they offered me was a good salary in those days and I accepted."[6]

In February of 1924, the Provincetown Players made public the fact that Paul would be the star in two of the Playhouse's productions. *The New York Times* promptly published a biographical sketch of Paul, describing the whole of his meritorious athletic career. After the announcement that Paul would play Jim in *All God's Chillun*, with the white actress Mary Blair playing black Jim's white wife, Ella, the play was published in *American Mercury* magazine for the public and critics to read.

But as soon as the play was published, conservative newspapers set up a storm of protest because, they said, the O'Neill play was advocating marriage between blacks and whites. In 1924, more than half of the forty-eight United States had laws forbidding marriage between the races. Today, such laws have largely been overturned. And while only a fraction of the public does intermarry, the question, "Would you want your daughter to marry a Negro?" has always been one of the irrational stumbling blocks to full equality of blacks in America.

On March 19, 1924, *The New York Times* headlined: "Author [Eugene O'Neill] Denies His Play of Negro's Marriage to White Woman Causes Ill Feeling." According to the *Times,* O'Neill "disclaimed all desire of presenting a theme which would cause racial ill feeling":

> I hate such feeling. It is because I am certain my play does not do this that I will stand by it to the end. I know I am right. I know that all the irresponsible gabble of the sensation-mongers and notoriety hounds is wrong. . . . All we ask is a square deal. . . . Mr. Robeson . . . can portray the character better than any other actor could. . . . A fine actor is a fine actor. The question of race prejudice cannot enter here.

Paul had accepted the role as Jim in *All God's Chillun,* he had said, because the part would pay money which he and Essie desperately needed. He would alternate this lead with playing the part of Brutus Jones in *The Emperor Jones.* Actually, Essie felt Paul took the roles because of the people involved in the Provincetown Players.

"They form one of the most intelligent, sincere, and non-commercial of the artistic groups in America," Essie wrote in 1930. "It is small wonder that when Paul Robeson came to work with them he fell under their spell."[7]

Indeed, it was true that for the first time, Paul was working with a group of whites who apparently had developed as artists without racial prejudice. Playwright Eugene O'Neill wrote significant plays that presented to the public a serious discussion of racial attitudes and discrimination. However, O'Neill never succeeded in completely rising above the prejudices of his time. In *All God's Chillun,* Ella becomes a prostitute and experiences a mental breakdown because of the conflicts caused by her marriage to black Jim. Jim is written as a good-natured, sentimental fellow, not many notches above the stereotyped "darky" of minstrel shows. Intellectuals of the Harlem Renaissance deeply resented the implications that only an insane white prostitute would marry a black man. And whites disliked the play because a white woman degrades herself before a black man. Though insane, at the end of the play Ella sits at Jim's feet while kissing his hand.

All God's Chillun certainly was an imperfect play with serious flaws. But it was the first attempt by an important theatrical company to produce a play starring a black in a human portrayal, and playing a leading role opposite a white woman.

The Emperor Jones was also highly unusual as drama. The lead character, Brutus Jones, is a pullman porter, an American black man. Almost immediately, the play takes on an unconventional form with an intended atmosphere of intense unreality. Written in eight scenes, it takes place on an island in the tropics where Brutus Jones has become dictator of the inhabitants. As the curtain rises, Jones is faced with a native uprising and has fled his palace to escape into the jungle. The islanders search for him while incessantly beating on drums. Gradually, the terrified emperor falls to pieces. And each scene finds him revealing more of his life and his black history through a panic-stricken "stream of consciousness" flow of words.

Brutus Jones had in the past boasted to the islanders that he could be killed only with silver bullets. Circling through the jungle, he returns to the place where he entered. There, he is shot with silver bullets by the chief of the natives.

Paul was very pleased to appear in both Province-

town Playhouse productions as it became apparent
that black people were proud that the famed Robeson
was being given the chance to show his race in so human a fashion. He would make his way downtown to
Greenwich Village from his Harlem apartment each
day. At the theater, author O'Neill waited with director James Light to teach Paul how to use to his advan-
tage his towering height and two-hundred-pound phy-
sique. Paul wasn't yet accomplished as an actor, but
without seeming to try, he carried somehow in his
very presence the sorrow of blacks living in white
America.

O'Neill and James Light intended to use all of
Paul's talent in order to produce the type of theater
drama they wanted. They added a black spiritual to
Paul's role in *The Emperor Jones,* and in both plays
tailored the parts to Paul's character, which they found
utterly noble in every respect. It was Paul's aloof but
proud self-confidence that appealed to O'Neill and
Light, and to intellectual whites at this time.

His size and his dark Bantu features brought to
mind all of the tragedy of slavery, as well as the memory of the African as a free man on his own continent.
As if these attributes weren't enough, he had the most
effortless, natural talent in three difficult fields. How
could he be anything but a winner?

Little did it matter that Paul didn't yet know what
the stakes were in order to win, or even what the
game would be. For the time, he had fallen under the
spell of the theater. And the theatrical world of
America had already made up its mind to fall in love
with him.

On opening night, May 15, 1924, Paul Robeson, actor, came to know the heady feeling of acclaim on the stage. For he was an immediate success in his role as Jim Harris in *All God's Chillun Got Wings*. There had been scattered attempts to stop the play from opening. The Ku Klux Klan, a secret organization of white supremacists, had sent threatening and obscene letters. But on opening night, the play progressed without incident to its conclusion, with the insane, white Ella sitting at black Jim's feet.

The audience loved Paul, and critic George Jean Nathan wrote in *American Mercury*, July 1924, that he "does things beautifully, with his voice, his features, his hands, his whole somewhat ungainly body, yet I doubt that he knows how he does them."

Nathan's comment was only partly correct. Director Light had been coaching Paul for weeks, but had limited his direction to technique that was natural to who and what Paul was.

The white public had become familiar with black singers and dancers. But never had they come upon a black actor such as Paul, who had such an uncommon aloofness, a sphere of quiet which he wore like a mantle on the stage. Here was this "colored" man, seemingly endowed with a hereditary gift—a kind of black genius which he projected to others from the depths of his personal and racial experience. He had grown to manhood at a time when the inner mood and artistic spirit of his people had come into its golden age.

And his ability to reveal that mood and spirit at will to others marked him as an intuitive actor.

Paul's performance in *The Emperor Jones* was also a forward step toward his career as a singer, since James Light had added a black spiritual to one scene in which Brutus Jones is lost in the jungle.

Paul grew to love singing and acting and thoroughly enjoyed the freedom his new life offered him. Throughout the months he was on stage in 1924 and the spring of 1925, he associated with the artists of the Provincetown Playhouse down in Greenwich Village. There were theater parties and shop talk in Village restaurants, about which Essie Robeson later wrote:

> There were many long, lazy, fascinating talks. Gene [Eugene O'Neill] had been nearly all over the world. . . . Paul would listen eagerly for hours, for days, for weeks. Meantime they worked on the plays. Jimmy [James Light] was vastly different from the usual director: he never told Paul what to do nor how to do it. He never told him what to say; he merely sat quietly in the auditorium and let him feel his way. . . .[1]

Obviously, James Light was a subtle director who knew the worth of Paul's natural ability. Paul was having a marvelous time, on the stage and off, in the Greenwich Village artists' and writers' area, where no one minded seeing the huge black fellow eating and laughing with Mary Blair, James Light and Eugene O'Neill.

Early in 1925, a black musical arranger and collector of the religious folk songs loosely termed Negro spirituals returned to the United States after a long self-exile in Europe. He was Lawrence Brown, and his reputation as a musician was growing, as was Paul's as an actor. He had met Paul in England in 1922 when Paul had played in the British production of *Taboo*. And now, by chance, they happened to meet again.

The ten blocks from 140th to 130th Street had become Paul's "beat." It took him hours to walk it because every few paces he was stopped by friends or acquaintances, and people who simply recognized him. He talked and strolled and became a landmark at 135th Street and Lenox Avenue, where Lawrence Brown caught sight of him. They warmly greeted one another, and later, at James Light's house, the two performed one of Lawrence Brown's arrangements of spirituals. James Light was so impressed by what he heard, that on the spot he talked them into giving a concert. There had never been a concert of spirituals and folk songs sung by one individual; such music was always arranged for choral groups. However, Light secured the Greenwich Village Theatre for the concert on April 19. Paul and Lawrence began at once to select songs, arranging them to fit Paul's voice and rehearsing for the performance. Thus, it happened that two gifted men, meeting by chance, got together to form what would become one of the most superb collaborations in musical history.

On the night of the concert, the theater was sold out to wealthy and well-dressed theater buffs. Even the standing room was sold. Out on the street, what few tickets to be had were being bought for twenty-five dollars apiece.

Everything had happened so quickly, Paul told Essie. It seemed like only yesterday that he'd run into Lawrence on 135th Street. Now, he faced another opening night. But this time, he would have his friend Lawrence with him.

The night of the concert, Paul sang "Go Down, Moses," "Joshua Fit de Battle of Jericho" and "Water Boy," among other songs. By the end of the program, he and Lawrence were exhausted, but the applause was breathtaking, with the audience screaming for more and more songs. And Paul sang with every ounce of his remaining strength to Lawrence's stirring piano accompaniment, and Brown joined in on many of the spirituals as a second voice.

The next day, *The New York Times* reviewed the

concert and captured its mood as well as the spirit of
the reviews from other New York papers:

> Mr. Robeson is a singer of genuine power. The
> voice is ample for his needs, mellow and soft, but
> it is his intense earnestness which grips his hearers.
> His negro spirituals have the ring of the revivalist,
> they hold in them a world of religious experience;
> it is this cry from the depths, this universal
> humanism, that touches the heart. . . . It was
> Mr. Robeson's gift to make them tell in every
> line, and that not by any outward stress, but
> by an overwhelming inward conviction. Sung
> by one man, they voiced the sorrows and hopes of
> a people.[2]

The review was a personal triumph for Paul. Just
twenty-seven years old, singing was a natural part of
his life as it was for a multitude of blacks who were
steady churchgoers in their chilhood and youth. For
as long as he could remember, he had been singing
and had had no special training. "If you think I have a
voice," he was fond of saying, "you should have heard
my father's!"

Yet, characteristically, Paul appeared untouched by
the clamor of his public and the praise of reviewers.
Perhaps his greater triumph was that he accepted his
own gifts as he did life itself. They were much like
breathing, or waking and sleeping. He lived with
them, each and every day.

In the winter of 1925–26, he and Lawrence signed
up to take their concert on tour. At the same time,
London's Ambassadors Theatre began negotiations
with the Provincetown Players to produce *The Emperor Jones*. For the English theater world had become aware of Paul Robeson.

Not since the middle of the nineteenth century had
a seasoned, black dramatic actor played the London
stage. At that time, Ira Aldridge had played Othello,
but there had not been a black actor of his stature in

the theater since. The name of Paul Robeson was virtually unknown to the general public in England when it was announced he would star in *The Emperor Jones* in London in September.

It hit Paul rather suddenly that for the first time in his life, his financial worries seemed to be at an end. He could make quite a good living singing or acting or both. And he and Essie sailed happily for England.

James Light was going to London to direct *The Emperor Jones* and Harold McGhee would go as the stage manager. All three men took their wives. The whole trip soon turned into a lark; once in London, the six of them settled in the Chelsea district, which had the flavor of their beloved Greenwich Village.

Paul grew to love London and spent much of his free time walking the city; gazing out on the Thames River; strolling the huge parks and squares. Life had an easy energy without the bustle and pace of New York.

Essie was to write about this time:

> There were few inconveniences for him [Paul] as a Negro in London. He did not have to live in a segregated district; . . . he ate at many other restaurants in town with his white or colored friends without fear of the discrimination which all Negroes encounter in America.[3]

"I think I'd like to live here," Paul told Essie; "some day I will."[4]

Actually, there was no lack of racial discrimination and class oppression in British life. But for the most part, these existed in far-off British colonies, such as India. Yet the Russian Revolution of 1917 had stimulated oppressed peoples throughout the world. And by the end of World War I, India was close to revolting against British rule. London may have appeared peaceful and serene, solid, for Paul freely strolling its streets. But in distant corners of the earth, the British Empire had begun to tremble.

As the time grew near for Paul's opening in *The Emperor Jones*, there was great excitement in London's theater world. The British colonial "Pukka sahibs" whose grandfathers had conquered India, and whose fathers were now its civil servants, thought a black man should never be given such prominence. However, most London theatergoers intended to turn out to see the "giant Negro."

In our age of seven-foot-tall basketball players, it seems odd that the six-foot-three Paul Robeson would be called a giant. But in the 1920's, few men were as much as six feet tall. Fewer still were over six feet, weighing more than 200 pounds, black and regal. Paul was all of these, with a most striking public presence.

He opened in *The Emperor Jones* on the night of September 11, and gave a stunning performance. Critics the following day spoke of his "remarkable presence and dignity and the richness and flexibility of his voice."

Yet it appeared that Paul didn't consider acting his most important talent. He told *The New York Times* covering his London opening:

> I want to sing—to show the people the beauty of negro folk songs and work songs. I will not go into opera, of course, where I would probably become one of the hundreds of mediocre singers, but I will concentrate on negro music, which has never been properly handled.[5]

He played Brutus Jones for a month, and while London critics lavished praise on him, he paid little attention to what they said. He knew he had no special acting ability, since it was his own innate self he expressed in every performance. So it was that with seeming modesty he remained disinterested in what critics had to say about him.

After the play had closed, Paul and Essie spent part of the winter on the French Riviera. They agreed that in England and France there were no apparent racial barriers against blacks. The fact was that the general public had not developed hard-and-fast anti-black attitudes that could be instituted as local policies of discrimination. Paul and Essie found no color bar in first-class restaurants or hotels. They saw no all-black, segregated communities, and there were few chances that they would ever be embarrassed publicly and turned away from entering an establishment, as they had often been in America. Neither of them was in any great hurry to return to their homeland. And they breathed the European air deeply, as though breathing freedom for the first time.

Meanwhile, across the ocean in America, the postwar decade brought only confusion. There were government scandals, anti-communist scares and eruptions of extreme patriotism. Historians would write:

> The Great Red Scare swept the country, labor unions were smashed, and the label of Bolshevism [Communism] was pinned on many progressively minded citizens. Outbreaks against the Jews, the Catholics, and the Negroes culminated in the revival of the Ku Klux Klan which exerted a demoralizing influence on community life. The fear that the "melting pot" was not working too successfully resulted in legislation severely limiting future immigration.[6]

Furthermore, great wealth appeared to have gone into partnership with government. The Republican Party in power used government to advance big business, as at this time there was a startling development in business monopolies. Ironically, this new white wealth financed many of the artists and playwrights of the Harlem Renaissance. And it helped to securely establish Paul Robeson on the stages of Europe and America.

Reluctantly, Paul and Essie came home in the winter of 1925–26 to prepare for a concert tour across the United States scheduled for Paul and Lawrence

Brown. Essie, having left her job at Columbia Presbyterian Medical Center to go to England, now became
their tour manager.

Paul sang such songs as "'Li'l David," "Didn't It
Rain?" and "Swing Low, Sweet Chariot" in his rich
baritone. As yet, the range of his voice wasn't spectacular, and its quality was still untrained. It was more
the selections of songs and the arrangements by Lawrence Brown that added greater dimension to Paul's
voice at this time. The power and strength of it were
there, but it had not yet developed into that instru-
ment of powerful emotion and depth by which it
would be remembered.

Elizabeth S. Sergeant wrote a remarkable article
about Paul in *The New Republic* on the third of
March, 1926. The article ran for four pages and revealed a growing adulation for Paul by his white, intellectual public:

> The singer's negroid features are more marked on
> the stage than off. His nose becomes a triangle of
> whiteness, his eyes white moons, his skin takes
> the milky lights that turn black into bronze. He
> has never seen a Georgia road gang but when he
> sings "Water Boy" the very accent and spirit of
> the Negro laborers enter into him and come out
> in that poignant vagrant song, one of the most
> beautiful in all folk music. Yet I have never seen
> on the stage a more civilized, a more finished and
> accomplished artistic gesture than his nod to his
> accompanist, the signal to begin the song. This
> gesture is the final seal of Paul Robeson's per-
> sonal ease in the world. Even a Southerner would
> have difficulty in negating its equality and el-
> bowing its creator from a sidewalk.[7]

While no "Southerner elbowed him off the side-
walk," Paul, Essie and Lawrence did experience constant, humiliating prejudice on their United States
tour. Paul couldn't have taken a room in any first-class

New York hotel between Greenwich Village and Harlem, a distance of more than one hundred blocks. He would not be given service in any first-class restaurant anywhere in the same area. If conditions seemed intolerable for him in New York City, they were far worse elsewhere in America.

He might walk from a concert in the finest music hall in the country, cross the street to a drugstore for a glass of water and be unceremoniously refused a drink. No single situation of their daily lives served to radicalize Paul and Essie more than these endless, petty incidents of racial discrimination and prejudice.

Such treatment was one of the reasons Essie began staying home in Harlem while Paul and Lawrence traveled in mid-1927. Moreover, she was going to have a baby.

Paul and Lawrence received frequent reviews in both the white and black press. Reviewers began to comment that Paul's baritone voice had gained in "smoothness and control."

In October of 1927, he returned to Europe and gave a concert in Paris. Again, *The New York Times* reviewers commented that Paul's voice, "which always has been highly regarded in America, is greatly improved in range and quality."

Although "highly regarded" in America, Paul was always much more acclaimed in Europe than at home. He and Lawrence continued with their highly successful European tour. At home in New York, Essie gave birth to a son on November 2, 1927; she named him Paul, Jr., called Pauli.

> Essie nearly lost her life in the struggle to bring him into the world. He was an exact replica of his father; the likeness was so startling that it became a joke among their friends. He was an enormous, healthy, happy, peaceful brown baby who grew more absurdly like his father as the months flew by. Even his baby voice was deep. No one ever

asked his name; everyone simply and naturally called him Paul.[8]

Paul returned from his tour deeply moved by the response of Europeans to his concerts. And he couldn't have been more pleased to have a son—and one that was the exact image of himself. Everything was perfect and became even more so when one day in April, he burst in on Essie:

"Come on, pack your things; we're going to London."

According to Essie, she thought he must be joking.

"Don't you believe it," Paul told her. "I'm going to sing 'Ol' Man River' in the London production of *Showboat*. It's all settled."

Essie was delighted to be leaving her homeland and returning to London. For a long time, she had been hurt deeply and had brooded about America's discrimination against blacks. It would be so good to get away. She left her son, Pauli, who was now five months old, in the competent hands of her mother, and she and Paul set sail for England.

On opening night at the Theatre Royal in Drury Lane in London, Paul acted the part of Joe in Jerome Kern and Oscar Hammerstein II's musical play *Showboat*. Just thirty years old, he played the role of a grey-haired, black, bending, middle-aged man who never ceased carrying bales of cotton from wharf to ship. Paul depicted the hard life of Joe and men like him, a life of drudgery that went on and on as the great, paddle-wheeled showboat stopped to entertain at towns along the Mississippi River. Joe seemed only a minor character as the musical, *Showboat*, proceeded through rehearsals. But something remarkable was to occur in Drury Lane that opening night in April.

As Joe, Paul Robeson straightened from his ceaseless toil to his towering height and began to sing the song of black men's pain and sorrow, of the river forever flowing free as black men never had:

* * *

Ah gits weary an' sick of try-in',
Ah'm tired of liv-in' an' skeered of dy-in'
But ol' man river,
He jus' keeps roll-in' a-long. *

As he finished "Ol' Man River," the audience at the
Theatre Royal sat stunned. They gazed openmouthed
at this man who had somehow clasped the history of
his people in his soul, and then had stepped out of
history in the guise of a performer in order to present
it to them. Suddenly, wave upon wave of applause
rose from the depths of the dimmed theater to thun-
der over him. Deeply moved by the wildly clapping
audience, he nevertheless remained in his role of Joe,
the son of slaves. Joe bent to his burden of toting
bales of cotton as the story of riverboat show people
continued.

Paul became an overnight sensation in London in
1928. Already known in New York theatrical circles,
and by the press, he was also a great sports figure of
whom black people could be exceedingly proud. Now,
he became famous all over England. Everyone was
talking about the "gigantic Negro" with his profoundly moving baritone voice. So much so, that the
manager of the Drury Lane theater began sponsoring
Sunday concerts featuring Paul, with Lawrence
Brown as accompanist. The concerts marked one of
the rare occasions when a member of a musical-
comedy cast became a solo artist in the very same
theater in which he performed each night.

Interest in *Showboat* stayed at a peak and the musical ran through the autumn and winter of 1928. Paul
and Essie became the "darlings" of the British upper
class. The parties they attended were noted in the
newspapers; society columnists talked about Essie

* "Ol' Man River" from the musical production *Showboat*.
Music by Jerome Kern. Lyrics by Oscar Hammerstein II. Copyright 1927 T. B. Harms Company. Copyright renewed. Used by
permission.

Robeson's fashionable clothes. Paul came to know such famed writers as H. G. Wells and the controversial Gertrude Stein. Stein wrote about him in her *Autobiography of Alice B. Toklas,* in which she pretends she is her friend, Miss Toklas, speaking:

> Paul Robeson interested Gertrude Stein. He knew american values and american life as only one in it but not of it could know them. And yet as soon as any other person came into the room he became definitely a negro. Gertrude Stein did not like hearing him sing spirituals. They do not belong to you any more than anything else, so why claim them, she said. He did not answer.[9]

Essie started work on a biography of Paul and in it she said that Paul's appeal to white women in Europe was causing problems in their marriage. However, she insisted that their love for one another was secure and that they would successfully overcome any discord:

> I know that you are faithful to me in the all important spirit of things; that I am the one woman in your life, in your thoughts, in your love. No matter what other women may have been to you, and you to them, they have in no way walked in my garden.[10]

In November, Paul was entertained in England's House of Commons at a luncheon and tea hosted by members of the Labor Party. Such honor was bestowed on him at a time when the American Embassy in London ignored the fact that he was in England at all. It was the Labor Party leader and former Prime Minister Ramsay MacDonald who arranged the luncheon for Paul and who engaged him in serious discussion about Britain's colonies.

At this time, Paul knew little about the British Labor Party or about socialism. But at the luncheon, he was quick to realize he was much in sympathy with the social equality views of MacDonald and other British Labor Party individuals.

Paul and Essie decided to stay in England after the run of *Showboat* ended. Essie's mother came over to England with Pauli, and they and Essie and Paul lived in Hampstead in a comfortable house overlooking the Heath.

Paul, who definitely had an ease with foreign languages, started his study of Chinese, and also German in order to sing German songs. He had begun learning Russian some years before. Also, he went on another highly successful concert tour in Vienna, Austria; Budapest, Hungary; and Prague, Czechoslovakia, where audiences shouted and stamped their feet in approval. Later on, when the tour was over, he began to rehearse for the lead role in Shakespeare's *Othello* and to study the English language of Shakespeare's time. The production, to open at the Savoy Theatre, would not be ready for about a year.

Between concerts and rehearsals, Paul sang at receptions and became a familiar figure in upper-class society. Yet even in England, he was to encounter problems because of his race.

Lady Sybil Colefax gave the Robesons a party at the Savoy Hotel Grill Room. When Paul and Essie arrived for the party, the hotel refused to let them in. This humiliating affront to the esteemed Robeson became overnight a public outrage. London newspapers carried the story. The Savoy Hotel, greatly embarrassed, announced that it didn't know how such an awkward mistake had been made! Finally, all major London hotels found it necessary to publicly state that they would not ever refuse to admit "Negroes." The public seemed satisfied to forget the incident. But how far must a man and woman travel through life before they can count on being treated as humans? It would never be erased from Paul's and Essie's memories.

Paul next went to America for a concert tour, which was quite well received by the public. Still, he encountered much more prejudice and discrimination in his homeland than he ever did in Europe. Often, people at home stared at him with barely concealed hostility. Many times, he was refused service in restaurants, and he never could be certain whether he could register at a hotel of his choice.

Such experiences made him extremely conscious of himself as a black man. He knew that artistic talent and the opportunity money brought isolated him from his own people, while at the same time, the blackness of his skin could unpredictably separate him from the white world.

Perhaps this was the reason he brought such unusual sensitivity to his role in *Othello*. Some claimed that Shakespeare's Moor was meant to be an Arab having no Negro blood; and others believed that Othello was distinctly negroid. The problem facing Paul was whether he could play the part as Shakespeare had meant it to be played. Finally, he decided that Shakespeare meant Othello to be a tragic figure because he was black and surrounded by whites. Thus, he told *The New York Times* on May 18, 1930:

I feel the play is so modern for the problem is the problem of my own people. It is a tragedy of racial conflict, a tragedy of honor, rather than of jealousy. Shakespeare presents a noble figure, a man of singleness of purpose and simplicity with a mind as direct as a straight line. He is important to the State but the fact that he is a Moor incites an envy of little-minded people. Desdemona loves him, he marries her, then the seed of suspicion is sown. The fact that he is an alien among white people makes his mind work more quickly. He feels dishonor more deeply. His color heightens the tragedy. . . . I am approaching the part as Shakespeare wrote it and am playing Othello as a man whose tragedy lay in the fact that he was sooty black.[11]

* * *

Paul had to be aware of the parallels between himself and Othello. Often, he had been made to feel "alien among white people" in his own country. If there were prophesy and tragedy awaiting him in the fact that he, too, like Othello, was "sooty black," then time would tell the tale.

By 1930, America was in the grip of a most over-whelming depression. Throughout the United States, starving, out-of-work people stood in lines for food and for jobs. The Wall Street stockmarket crash of October and November 1929 had started this Great Depression, the single most devastating crisis to overwhelm America since the Civil War. The crisis quickly spread out from the business of high finance to heavy industry, and from America outward to include the rest of the world.

The depression broke wide open in England while Ramsay MacDonald was prime minister in a Labor-Party dominated coalition government. Immediately, unemployment leaped from the million mark to over three million.

Yet well-to-do Londoners lined up outside the Savoy Theatre to see Paul Robeson in the stage production of *Othello*. The play starred Maurice Browne as Iago, Dame Peggy Ashcroft as Desdemona and, of course, Paul as Othello. It was a magnificent production in its pageantry and movement. And Paul was majestic in his love for Desdemona. He was equally terrifying in his rages, not of jealousy, but of moral despair.

At the end of the opening night performance, the audience rose to its feet, cheering and crying, "Robeson! Robeson!" There were twenty curtain calls, with the crowd continuing the clamor until Paul came forward to express his happiness.

London critics vied with one another to see who

could give *Othello* the most praise. However, some reviews, typified by the one in the *Morning Post* the next day (May 30, 1930), were a curious combination of praise and condescension:

> There is, of course, no need to apologize for Mr. Robeson because he is a Negro. Though in conventional grace and some niceties of diction we have had English Othellos from whom he might learn, there has been no Othello on our stage, certainly in forty years, to compare with his in dignity, simplicity and true passion. He made the part sympathetic and appealing, not only because he was more real, but also because together with his deep, virile voice there was a childlike racial simplicity that made Othello's submission to Iago's suggestions understandable and the "pity of it" not only poignant but also logical. The slight American accent is a trouble at first, but one soon gets used to this. In general, from an elocutionary point of view, one only wishes some of our actors could take example from his rolling and natural response to the rhythm and beauty of Shakespeare's verse.

American newspapers, including *The Christian Science Monitor* and *The New York Times*, took note of the London production of *Othello*. There was soon talk of producing the play in the United States, with Paul in the lead. Immediately, the old, dull racial question arose, that of showing on the stage a racially mixed sexual relationship. White Desdemona and black Othello kiss and embrace in the play in a love situation that was considered shocking and distasteful to most American whites. There began a strong argument against presenting the play in New York. And although the talk was stupid and disgusting, it was serious enough as a countermove to put an end to all plans to stage *Othello* at home.

In London, Paul was well aware of what was happening in New York. On May 22, *The New York Times* carried an article stating that "Negro Who Kisses White Girl on London Stage Would Expect Protest in America." Paul had said in the interview:

> They certainly wouldn't stand in America for the kissing and for the scene in which I use Miss Ashcroft roughly. I wouldn't care to play those scenes in some parts of the United States. The audience would get rough; in fact, might become very dangerous.[1]

But the question of his altering the role of Othello was now academic. Because of racial fear and prejudice, there would be no New York production of the play until thirteen years later.

Although Paul was still something of an oddity to many in London— a curiously talented giant of a Negro—he was increasingly recognized as an important actor and not solely as a representative of a race. On Sundays, he and Lawrence performed a program of entertainment at the Savoy, so popular had he become from his Othello role. He played scenes from *The Emperor Jones* and sang black spirituals. *The New York Times* dutifully reported the program for the public. And while praising Paul, it made an outrageous statement concerning the spirituals:

> The success of the experiment that Paul Robeson is making this week at the Savoy Theatre is proof of his complete acceptance by the London public. The whole entertainment depends upon him. It begins and ends with two groups of Negro songs and its centre is the first act of *The Emperor Jones.* . . . Negro spirituals are, as a form of art, of so little value that it is hard to make them sustain an evening in the sophisticated circumstances of a theatre. . . . They make little appeal to the mind.[2]

*   *   *

Obviously, the *Times* was not willing to accept Paul on his own terms, as a black artist pridefully exhibiting and defining the finest folk art of his people. Yet England certainly was, and Paul's popularity continued to rise. Women had always made a fuss over him and now became seriously involved in his personal life. He and Essie separated in 1930. She stayed in England but lived away from Paul with little Pauli and her mother. Essie involved herself in problems of blacks in England and the mother continent, Africa, and studied anthropology at the London School of Economics. She was very interested in putting her ideas about race and economics into action and was not terribly concerned with political party affiliations. Neither was Paul at this time, for he was completely absorbed in his personal career and in his own black problem.

Essie's biography of Paul, entitled *Paul Robeson, Negro*, was published in 1930 by Harper & Brothers, New York. In the first week of August, it was reviewed extensively by *The New Republic*. And the magazine was devastating in its condemnation of Essie's book:

> Difficulties there have no doubt been, certainly enough at times to hurt a sensitive spirit, but to distort such facts is to make of Paul Robeson a remarkable Negro instead of what he is, a remarkable man. . . . The biography written by his wife does much, a good deal more perhaps than she knows, to despoil his legend.[3]

Apparently, *The New Republic* took issue with the fact that Essie depicted Paul's life and that of his father before him as a difficult one, with emphasis on that which was uniquely black in their lives. One senses that the magazine did not like her candor. For instance, Essie mentions that ticket sellers often mistook her for white because of her fair skin. She wrote freely of what she suspected were Paul's love affairs. And she must have shaken the white friends of the Harlem Renaissance when she wrote about whites visiting Harlem:

> If the sight-seers are Southerners come to "see how these No'thern niggers live in this Harlem they talk so much about," the Negroes in the streets immediately sense this, and shout mockingly to no one in particular:
> "Lordy, Rastus, some mo' white folks lookin' fo' Mammy, an' Uncle Tom, an' Ol' Black Joe." If the white visitors are sophisticated slummers, they go directly to Small's, or Connie's Inn, or some similar night club in Harlem which is maintained almost exclusively for white patronage.[4]

The biography was written in a bubbly, enthusiastic style. Essie wrote about herself and Paul in the third person, as shown in this section concerning the baby, Paul, Jr.:

> One morning when the Robesons were breakfasting in their home in Hampstead, their small son, Paul, junior, came in. Mrs. Goode, his grandmother, beamed. She secretly thought Paul saw far too little of his baby, and that he was strangely lacking in interest in the child. "Ah," she said, pleased at finding them, "good morning, son. And here is *your* son." She turned to the baby, a small, brown, sturdy, adorable rascal, ridiculously like his father. "Say good morning to Daddy." Large Paul looked bored and tried to conceal his irritation. Small Paul did not even hear his grandmother; he was gazing at the table with eager eyes. "Cweam, suyar, coffee," he said, and let go the full charm of his smile, dimples, and baby teeth upon his mother, hoping she would allow him to put lumps of sugar carefully into her cup, and guide his fat hand while he poured in the cream.[5]

* * *

In any case, Essie began to be known as a writer and considered herself as such. And in the meantime, Paul's success brought him the opportunity to be one of the few Americans to be listed in the *Who's Who* of Britain. In an ambiguous tone, *The New York Times* reported in December: "It must be assumed that Paul Robeson, the Negro actor-singer, is included largely because of his popularity in Britain. . . . It is worthy of note that he is not even included in his own country's *Who's Who*."[6]

The great sculptor Jacob Epstein sculpted Paul's head in tribute to his superb artistry. Paul's experimental program with Lawrence Brown at the Savoy was polished enough now to take on tour. And as always, his singing moved audiences far more than did his acting. Yet in all of this time, he had no clear-cut purpose. Often, after having received ovation upon ovation for a fine performance, he would go quietly home to read or study languages.

For there was no more indescribable suffering for Paul than his emotional state during this period of his great public acclaim and his private humiliation. The early 1930's revealed his steady mastery of his art, and his continued fame as an individual artist on concert tours in England and in the United States. But in the U.S., unrecognized in small towns, Paul was the object of prejudice and discrimination as was the rest of his race.

He could never quite come to terms with this splitting of himself down the middle. For on the one hand, he was the great singer and actor to be praised; on the other, he was a black treated as an inferior because of his skin. Furthermore, he made large sums of money, while millions of men like him starved to death in the Depression in America. No wonder then that he rushed home to be alone after many a concert; he worried constantly about his place in the world.

In these years, Paul had come to know the Russian language and he spoke German rather well. Moreover, he busily studied French, which helped to enrich and expand his repertoire of songs. After his tour with Lawrence, he portrayed the huge, hairy ship's stoker in the London production of *The Hairy Ape* by Eugene O'Neill. He next portrayed Joe in a revival of *Showboat* in New York, the first time that he sang the role of Joe for theater audiences at home.

But Paul's life as a person, as an individual, remained in England:

> He felt that he understood the British people and felt himself to be part of the English scene. . . . As the country became more and more a part of him, he felt a new kind of individualism asserting itself within him, one that seemed to have no race or nationality; a consciousness neither black nor white but of the world.[7]

In England and on the continent, he saw himself as the son of a former slave who could live as a man. He could educate his own marvelous little son without having him suffer racial indignities. He felt comparatively free and he told everyone that England was his home.

A year after the run of *Showboat* in New York, Paul and Essie seemed to have resolved their differences. Family problems were somehow taken care of and Paul came home to Hampstead and Essie. He was, perhaps, a somewhat different man now. He was much more sophisticated. And having moved freely among the upper class of London, he made a startling discovery. English aristocrats treated their white servants with the same disregard as whites in America treated blacks. So apparent and simple an observation deeply upset Paul. But slowly, he began to ponder the problem of economic class and became more conscious of society in general and of the poor of many races in particular. Concert tours in 1929 had first brought him into contact with poverty in Europe and the wretched plight of Jews on the continent.

But despite his growing perception and understanding, he didn't want to bring attention to himself for reasons of race or politics, or to "make speeches . . . about what they call the Colour Question while I can sing."[8] Old dreams still had hold of him. For he had always wanted to go to Germany and to live there for a time, to study the language and music more extensively.

But Adolph Hitler became Chancellor of Germany at the beginning of 1933 and declared himself the voice of the German people. "Pure" Germans, he said, must depend solely on one another and on a strong leader, himself, and on his Nazi Party, who had their interests at heart. He spoke out against German Marxists, communists, and social democrats, and deliberately confused the politics of each. He established a dictatorship with control over the political, economic and cultural life of the people, with himself as Führer, or Leader. He denounced the Jews as "impure" people.

Thousands of Jews fled from Nazism and streamed into London. What few possessions they carried with them had been snatched from them by Nazi border guards. Suddenly, England was filled with poor, starving foreigners who swelled the depression ranks of the unemployed and the hungry.

Paul was appearing in the London production of *All God's Chillun Got Wings*, the O'Neill play in which an interracial marriage had caused such controversy in the United States. And now, people who had known him as a black man of depth and of emotion came to him on behalf of Jewish refugees. A committee headed by the writer H. G. Wells was formed to aid the refugees. On the committee were such socially conscious individuals as Marie Seton, the author who would years later write a biography of Paul. Miss Seton and others of the committee hoped to persuade the producers of *All God's Chillum* to give a benefit for the refugees.

Paul at first refused to play the benefit on the

grounds that he would be taking sides in a matter of politics! He said, "I don't understand politics. . . . My province is art."[9] He had had little time to pay attention to international politics and had only a sketchy understanding of what was happening. Years later, he told Miss Seton that he "didn't realize it was the end of democracy in Germany." But the plight of Jewish refugees struck a sympathetic chord in him. For Paul had said more than once that "the white people who have been kindest to me in America have been Jewish people."[10]

It wasn't very long before Paul agreed to play the benefit. And in so doing, he made one of his most important decisions on the way to political awareness. His politics were always pure in their simplicity. He simply believed in the equality of man, and he was now willing to take risks for this belief.

The benefit for the refugees raised some two thousand pounds sterling to aid them. For Paul, it had raised his consciousness, demonstrating to him that the inferior status of Jews in Germany was not unlike that of blacks in the United States of America.

In May of 1933, Paul was back in New York to star in the movie of *The Emperor Jones* adapted from the O'Neill play. The independent production was released by United Artists; and Paul, playing Brutus Jones, received fine notices in the newspapers. Yet the movie had little relevance for black people fighting through the Great Depression for freedom as well as food and jobs. DuBose Heyward, the adapter, had created a new set of characters for the film, who were not much more than outlandish stereotypes of blacks. Some of the scenes of crime in a black underworld served only to reinforce the generalization by whites that blacks were stupid, wild and criminal. When Paul had undertaken to act in the film, he had had no idea it would be so radically changed from the play.

However, the film did open doors for Paul in America. The press and the public were ever more friendly to him. He was a guest artist on radio for the National

Broadcasting Company, singing such old favorites as "Water Boy" and "Ol' Man River" to millions of Americans.

By August, he was back in London, tired but happy with the success of his American trip. He had changed greatly and was still changing. A short while before, he had wanted to live in Germany, to sing German songs, to know the German language. While he was still interested in the language, all the rest had changed. Nazism, anti-Semitism, the plight of Jewish refugees, had made him sensitive to world affairs. And still changing, still growing, he was now willing to discuss the "Colour Question." He didn't want to be only an individual, he wanted to be a black individual furthering the cause of blackness as well as working-classness. Thus, he went beyond his repertoire of black folk music and spirituals to include folk music of Mexico, Russian songs, and Irish, Finnish and South American music. He continued his study of languages and acquired a knowledge of African Yoruba, Efik, Benin and Ashanti, as well as some Chinese and Arabic. Paul had a special affinity for Russian; he could speak it well now and he could sing it with almost native feeling that was truly inspiring.

Essie and Paul soon moved to London, where they took an apartment. Young Pauli attended school in Austria for a while and then in Switzerland. Essie continued her studies and her writing. Paul studied singing, languages and Africa. He felt a new surge of enlightenment when he had acquired some background knowledge of the African continent:

> It is my ambition to guide the Negro Race by means of its own peculiar qualities to a higher degree of perfection along the lines of its natural development. . . . These qualities and attainments of Negro [i.e., African] languages are entirely unknown to the general public of the Western world and, astonishingly enough, even to Negroes themselves. I have met Negroes in the

U.S. who believed that the African Negro communicated his thoughts by means of gestures, . . . that . . . he was practically incapable of speech and merely used sign language.[11]

Paul became well acquainted with African students who always turned out for his London concerts. They looked on him as a true African, with his dark skin and Bantu features. Such young men as Kwame Nkrumah and Jomo Kenyatta, who would one day be the leaders of their own independent nations, looked at him with awe.

Many African students were coming to study in England in the middle 1930's as their continent began to catch up with modern life. They formed a West African Students' Union and made Paul and Essie Robeson honorary members. These African students associated with other dark-skinned students from the West Indies, Asia and India. They regularly came out to hear Paul sing, and many saw him as the perfect representative of what was fine and black.

Paul had become a celebrated black for white radicals, also. On English university campuses, socialist clubs expounding the philosophy of complete racial equality were very popular. He was their prime example of successful racial freedom; and he was invited to speak at the Socialist Club of Cambridge University, even though he had not yet made public a political point of view. But for student socialists, Paul didn't need to say a word. He *was* the symbol of emerging darker peoples and clearly a new man bringing forth a new society.

Early in 1934, Paul and Lawrence Brown had taken part in a wide-ranging Celebrity Concerts tour in Scotland, and in English towns. There were quite a number of celebrities involved in this tour, but it was always Paul and Lawrence who pulled the largest crowds. With his expanded repertoire of songs, Paul filled music halls with the most enthusiastic audiences ever seen.

By the summer, he was again making a movie. He portrayed Bosambo, a tribal chief in the film version of Edgar Wallace's book *Sanders of the River*. When Paul later went to work on retakes, he found that new scenes had been added without his knowledge. To his astonishment, *Sanders of the River* now sang the praises of British colonialism. Bosambo was grateful to his "white masters" and loyal only to Sanders, played by Leslie Banks, who was the film's white man carrying the "white man's burden."

Paul was furious at having been duped; yet he had signed a contract which gave him no right to reject the completed film script.

The *Sanders* film opened at the Leicester Square Theatre as a story of colonial rule. After the showing, Paul, sitting agonized in the audience, was asked to come on stage and say a few words. He did stand, to his powerful height. But his face was contorted with rage. He stalked out of the theater, not saying a word and never looking back.

Sanders of the River had been a humiliating experience for Paul. And a year later in the New York *Amsterdam News*, he attempted a defense for playing Bosambo:

> To expect the Negro artist to reject every role with which he is not ideologically in agreement, is to expect the Negro artist under our present scheme of things to give up his work entirely.[12]

However, some good came out of his *Sanders* work. The great Russian film director Sergei Eisenstein heard about Paul and read about him making movies. Eisenstein wanted Paul to portray the life of Haitian liberator Toussaint L'Ouverture. He contacted an acquaintance, writer Marie Seton, and asked her help in persuading Paul to come to Russia for discussions about the film project. Miss Seton was happy to help in any way she could. And on December 20, 1934, *The New York Times* announced that Paul would make a

visit to the "Soviets," a trip he had been eagerly awaiting. The *Times* went on to say that in the next year,
"Robeson plans to go to Africa to determine the possi-
bilities of establishing a Negro homeland, such as Pal-
estine for the Jews."

Actually, what Paul had said, while addressing the
League of Colored People of London, was that black
Americans should restore to their own history their
African heritage. Other newspapers reported that Paul
was going to Africa because he had given up on Western civilization. He would most certainly go to Africa
some day but first he would go to Russia. He had
heard from black students in London about what was
going on in the Soviet Union. Famed West Indian poet
of the Harlem Renaissance Claude McKay was an old
friend of Paul's, and he had been in the Soviet Union
several times. McKay never stopped talking about the
improvements in social justice he had seen there. For
to him and others, the Soviet Union meant freedom
and equality for the mass of mankind.

It wasn't difficult for Paul to contrast what he
heard about economic progress in the Soviet Union
with the worldwide depression—millions unemployed,
factories shut down. These, his friends told him, were
the terrible ills of capitalistic democracy. He listened
closely, with a growing need to understand the world
and to reach for a broader purpose than that of a professional actor. So it was that no trip would so completely awaken him as the one to the Soviet Union,
nor create the conditions through which he would become a political man.

Paul and Essie went to Russia at the height of world Depression. At home in America, some 13,000,000 people were out of work. Thousands took to the highways and railroads, starving, wandering, seeking a way to survive. They died by the hundreds of disease and exposure. Tarpaper-and-tin shantytowns sprang up overnight in the countryside and at the edge of cities. President Franklin Roosevelt had said in his first inaugural address the year before, "The only thing we have to fear is fear itself." And at once he launched his threefold New Deal program of relief, recovery and reform.

Lying directly across the North Pole from a stunned and devastated American was the Soviet Union, covering one sixth of the land area of the earth, two and a half times larger than the U.S., with the longest frontiers in the world. Within its borders, a hundred peoples spoke as many languages. In 1922, the Union of Soviet Socialist Republics was established as a way of solving the age-old problem of discontented Russian nationalism. The federal structure, many socialist republics in one Union, was conceived in order to give self-respect, equality and the spirit of cooperation to Russian minorities. The Union furthermore was hoped to be the first step in uniting workers of all countries into one World Soviet Socialist Republic. The Third Communist International had taken place in 1919. Called the Comintern, it was a gathering of workers' organizations and Marxists from all over the world who accepted "revolution as in Russia, socialization of property as in Russia, application of Marxism* as in Russia."[1] The Comintern attempted to refute *moderate* socialism; and those socialist parties that would follow Comintern policies dropped the name "Socialist" and thereafter called themselves Communist.

Paul and Essie Robeson left England in December 1934, for their long journey to the Soviet Union. They would pass through Germany, where they expected to see all of the pageantry of the Christmas season. However, Germany's suffering was also very great during the economic collapse of the world. As in other parts of Europe, factories were shut tight; millions were unemployed. A stream of leaders had governed in a state of emergency until 1933, when Adolph Hitler became Chancellor of Germany. The Nazi (National Socialist German Workers' Party) Revolution had begun, with its Führer denouncing unearned incomes, great trusts, chain stores and, above all, Jews. Hitler termed his revolution or new order the Third Reich (Empire), which he said would last a thousand years.

Paul and Essie entered Germany in the second year of the Third Reich, at a time when Hitler had already taken Austria into his Reich.

---

* This system of thought is codified in *The Communist Manifesto*, the first statement of the tenets of modern communism, written by Karl Marx with Friedrich Engels in 1848. But Soviet Marxism, developed by Vladimir Lenin and later modified by Joseph Stalin, became the system of thought of the Soviet Union.

Joseph Stalin, as Secretary General of the Communist Party Central Committee from 1922 until his death in 1953, had supreme power for his dictatorship. He simplified Marxism-Leninism in the Soviet Union, and through ruthless action, defined it. Stalin believed, as had Lenin before him, that it was possible to have communism in one country without waiting for the support of worldwide revolution. But unlike Lenin, what counted most for Stalin was "the immediate goal, the practical result." This course led to the intensification of the class struggle within the Soviet Union and a policy of repression and terror.

In 1928, Joseph Stalin organized Soviet industralization in a succession of five-year plans. The result of these plans was an extraordinary upheaval—in effect, a powerful new Russian revolution.

The Robesons had time to spend only one day in Berlin in order to make connections with their train to the Soviet Union. And Miss Seton, who was familiar with Moscow, joined them by the next train. Paul had visited Germany once before. Just four years earlier, in 1930, he had played in *The Emperor Jones* in Berlin at stage-and-screen director Max Reinhardt's theater there. Now, Reinhardt had fled from the Third Reich, as had most of Paul's other German friends.

Paul was always tremendously conscious of the atmosphere around him, Marie Seton later wrote.* As he and Essie and Miss Seton left the train station for their hotel, he was painfully aware of the looks people gave him. Most turned quickly away from noticing him—a huge black.

Racism was there in the air Paul breathed as he walked quickly toward his hotel. He had known it too often in the past at home not to recognize it now in Berlin. Brownshirted storm troopers were everywhere. They stared at him with pure hatred as they brushed arrogantly past him.

Once at his hotel, he refused to leave the room again until a few hours before train time. Essie thought it might calm him if she telephoned a Jewish friend of his whom he had known in 1930. Obligingly, the man came around to the hotel, only to make matters worse. Furtively, he talked of Nazism and the concentration camps of the Third Reich. Obviously fearing to become somehow trapped in the hotel, the friend soon left.

Paul began pacing up and down, back and forth, until he had marked the exact dimensions of an invisible cage. He could no longer stand the room, he said. And so he and Essie and Miss Seton hurried out to a movie, which ironically turned out to be a travelogue on Africa. It was dark by the time they came out of the theater and headed for the station. But they were

* Miss Seton is the sole source for the following anecdotal material.

still a half hour early for their train. Miss Seton wrote
vividly of what then took place:

> Essie went to collect our luggage and Paul and I
> went to find the train. But it had not come in and
> the platform was almost deserted except for scat-
> tered stormtroopers. We stood talking. Suddenly
> Paul's body grew tense; his words slowed down
> and the blood flushed into his face. "Keep on
> talking as if you haven't noticed anything," he
> said abruptly.[2]

Storm troopers gathered to form a line between
Paul and Miss Seton and other passengers on the train
platform:

> Each Nazi was staring at us. In his belt, each had
> a revolver and the crooked black cross in the
> white square [sic] on the blood-red band glared
> from each arm. Paul went on talking, slowly, de-
> liberately and we edged closer to one another.
> First one brownshirt, than another muttered an
> epithet.[3]

The storm troopers began cursing Paul in German.
Paul knew what was happening. If he or Miss Seton
showed any fear, the incident could escalate into a
lynching right here in Berlin, just as it might in Mississippi.

Essie, who had been hunting baggage, returned
without it. Immediately, another line of brownshirts
gathered behind her.

For a moment, she couldn't imagine what was going
on. Then, it became appallingly clear to her. This was
the nightmare, dark and unutterable, that every black
fears he may one day have to live: Helpless and alone,
he will die the most dreaded and despised of deaths.

There was a tense silence, then shouts and curses at
Essie and Miss Seton. Suddenly, Paul heard the train.

It had reached the platform and he hurried the two women aboard. Miraculously, their baggage came at the very last moment; it was thrown on. Paul got on. No Nazi made a move to stop him as the train pulled away. And somberly, he took a last look at the future Germany in the contorted faces of storm troopers, a Germany in which hatred would triumph.

For hours he sat staring out at the night. Later, he talked a little but not much. "I never understood what Fascism was before," he said.[4] And he vowed to fight it.

The dangerous moments on the train platform did much to complete the changes going on inside him. The artist searching for his individual place in the world merged with the man who would never retreat from injustice. After Berlin, Paul's political point of view crystalized and he was bound to fight intolerance wherever he found it. But he still believed in what he termed a black renaissance of art and culture, distinct from that of white, Western civilization. Paul did not overnight become a political man. However, he could not have gone to Russia at a more opportune time.

America had officially recognized the USSR in 1933. There was warm feeling in Russia for American citizens, black citizens in particular. Moreover, the Union was gaining a place in the sun and becoming a symbol of equality for those colonized African and Asian peoples who still lived under European rule.

At the Soviet border station, passport officers told Paul that he and Essie would have to return to London because their visas were not in order. Someone thought to place a call to Intourist, the Soviet tourist agency in Moscow. As all waited for word to come, Paul took out his record player and some of his records which he had brought along. When the officers heard Paul's baritone, they knew at once who he was. It was the music and voice of "Pavel Robesona," and he was already known and loved in the Soviet Union.

Surprised and pleased, Paul spoke to everyone in fluent Russian. The problem with the passports was soon worked out and the Robeson party was graciously put on the train to Moscow. They were to stay in the Soviet Union for two weeks as the guests of famed film director Sergei Eisenstein. When they reached Moscow, Mr. Eisenstein and a number of other people waited to greet them.

From the first day, Paul met Russians and non-Russians with equal grace and ease; and he was always amazed to find how well known he was. He met foreigners, a black actor who was studying with Eisenstein, and he met many Chinese studying in Moscow. How very different was his reception here from what it had been in Germany! He talked to everyone and was greeted by people all over Moscow. Russians exclaimed over his size and height as he freely, endlessly strolled the streets, with Eisenstein at his side.

Paul learned about the Soviet educational system which instructed its students that no one was to be made to feel inferior because of race or color. The folkways and nationalism of individual groups were tolerated and not completely submerged. But the Soviet Union had so many racial groups that color prejudice had to be systematically eradicated. Universities were established where ethnic toleration became highly visible as examples of Soviet equality. One such school was the University of Toiling People of the Far East, which served students from India, Africa and the Near East. The school was in no way exclusively Communist; many of the students here were the sons and daughters of working-class families who were unable to obtain education in their own countries.

Aware of the oppressed condition of blacks at home, Paul was deeply impressed by what he saw. "I hesitated to come," he told Eisenstein. ". . . I didn't think this would be any different for me than any other place. But . . . I feel like a human being for the first time since I grew up. Here I am not a Negro but a human being. . . . You cannot imagine what that means to me as a Negro."[5]

Blacks in Moscow all said that there was no discrimination in the Union and that they were treated as equals. Paul met William L. Patterson, a black lawyer also visiting Moscow. Patterson, as Secretary of the American Civil Rights Congress, was involved in the Scottsboro Case and the defense of nine Alabama youths who were accused of raping two white women. He had aligned himself with American Communist Party beliefs in the Scottsboro defense. Paul regarded Mr. Patterson as a well-educated black man who was attempting to improve the condition of all blacks. Patterson urged Paul to come home, where his talents and the high esteem in which the public held him could only aid the black cause.

Could he do that? How could he go home? Paul wondered. At home, race hatred had been the cause of his humiliation so many times. He knew only too well the condition of poor, deprived blacks, for he had once been poor and deprived, himself. He couldn't, he wouldn't identify himself with a country that deprived its largest minority of human equality.

The Soviet Union appealed to his deep and abiding sense of the equality of man. He daily witnessed the fact that it accepted black Americans for their own worth, as it accepted nonwhites within its own population. Russians, both men and women, threw their arms around him and kissed him. The Soviet Foreign Minister, Maksim Litvinov, had a huge Christmas dinner with turkey, wine and caviar. Paul sang black spirituals, danced and was very very gay. Everywhere, Paul sang—at the Kaganovitch ball-bearing plant, for Eisenstein's film crews on Christmas Day. Always, when he sang, Russians looked on with awe at this giant black man and stood to applaud him.

When Russian children saw him, they ran after him, screaming with pleasure, and flung themselves upon him. They looked up at him as if he were some magical giant. Of course, they were amazed by the darkness of his skin. But Paul exuded charm. It was his smiling, friendly face that moved them to show such open affection. And he was quick to realize that here was a fine country in which to raise his son, Pauli.

However, there were some hard and terrifying realities of Soviet life not always apparent. Landowners and well-off peasants who resisted the collectivization of their farms (under the Five-Year Plan 1928–33, the Collectivization of Agriculture) were systematically annihilated or sent away to far-off labor camps for the rest of their lives. Moreover, Communist Party leader Joseph Stalin purged the Party of opponents, forcing them to "confess" real or suspected acts of disloyalty to the communist revolution.

Millions of the poorer peasants now worked the new collective farms, where they ceased to starve for the first time in generations and where they were introduced to education and modern agricultural techniques. In the Eastern Soviet Republics, nonwhite nationalities were freed from the serfdom they had experienced under the czars.

The Soviet system exemplified an unsentimental, even ruthless, revolution, in which those who defied it were destroyed. But the Union had made the assumption that its masses of downtrodden peoples had the right to enjoy the fruits of their own labors, and to live free of the tyranny of the wealthy and wellborn. It was an astounding assumption that fascinated the world in which it had long been believed that the poor had few rights, least of all the right to a decent life. Historians were to write that:

> Socialism [i.e. Communism] . . . did away with some of the evils of unrestrained free enterprise. There was no unemployment. There was no cycle of boom and depression. There was no such misuse of women and children as in the early days of industrialism in the West. There was no absolute want or pauperization, except for political undesirables, and except for temporary conditions of

famine. There was a minimum below which no
one was supposed to fall.[6]

For Paul Robeson, the Soviet Union appeared to be
the place he had been searching for for most of his
life. Russian people accepted him as a man as well as
an artist. They didn't concern themselves about his
color and he thought very little about their Communism. What he saw in them was the practice of human
equality,* and he would never ever forget what he
saw.

* In 1936, the Soviet Union instituted a new constitution in
which all forms of racism were condemned. Its citizens were
given rights beyond the civil rights found in democracies, such
as economic security, steady employment, leisure, a secure old
age.

After a profoundly moving and happy visit, Paul and Essie left Moscow for London on January 6, 1935. Paul was now prepared to change the course of his life. He and Essie planned not to spend much time in the United States or England. They hoped to spend part of every year in the Soviet Union, and they would go to Africa in the next year. They had been invited to Uganda by a friend, the cousin of the Prince of Toro, and Essie had decided to complete her research work in anthropology in various parts of Africa.

As for the Soviet Union, Paul told reporters that he knew very little about Communist economics or politics. But he did admire the way the people lived, the way they treated one another and foreigners, too.

Sergei Eisenstein wanted Paul to start in *Black Majesty,* his projected film study of Toussaint L'Ouverture. They had discussed the project before Paul left. But Paul found that he wouldn't be free to make the picture until the fall because he was committed to play in a production entitled *Stevedore* in London during the summer.

In April 1935, he began rehearsals for *Stevedore* at the Embassy in London. He threw himself whole-heartedly into the production because he felt that this play would show blacks in a light that was right and just.

In the play, Lonnie Thompson, a militant dock worker described in Act I as a "bad nigger," is eventually framed by the criminal mob. Lonnie, portrayed by Paul, dies heroically defending his union and his people. And at the end of the play, the mob is stoned by both white and black dockhands, who realize at last that they must fight together. One can't help wondering if this was meant to show the equality of violence. In any case, the scene was so real and emotional that during one performance, well-known tap dancer Bill Robinson climbed onto the stage and took his place with the rock-throwing dockhands!

Paul believed *Stevedore* to be an important play because it showed a black laborer with a strong racial feeling for his people but an equally strong feeling for his class, symbolized by his union. It opened in May to mixed reviews, the play being described by reviewers as uneven and incomplete. However, Paul was given exceptionally good notices. And he was happy that his acting was developing at a pace with the shaping of new ideas within him. For once, the role he played—even though flawed—and he himself were expressing the same ideals. Adding to his happiness was the fact that he soon would be making a movie, the right kind of movie about blacks and Africa, called *Song of Freedom*.

Paul had hoped to get back to Moscow and Eisenstein in the fall, but by that spring, Eisenstein had begun to work on another picture. The opportunity to make *Black Majesty* was lost. Paul was sorry not to be able to visit the Soviet Union again. It had been much on his mind and he had begun slowly to focus his attention on the theory and practice of race equality there. He had begun to investigate the classic works of Marxism, the system of modern socialism developed by Karl Marx with Friedrich Engels.

For a time, Paul made himself unavailable to friends and for engagements by not answering letters or telephones. But he would talk to scholars or anyone else who knew something about the Soviet Union. He met and talked with Britain's authority on Soviet economics, Andrew Rothstein. He talked with the West Indian George Padmore, who had made a study of Soviet minorities. Moreover, he carefully studied the folk music of peoples over the earth with his new insight of Marxism.

But by the latter part of 1935, he was again answering his mail and phone and accepting invitations to sing or act. He agreed to go to the United States for his first concert tour in three years and to play Joe the riverman in a film production of *Showboat*. He would be seeing his son, Pauli, with whom he had spent so little time. Pauli had left England because of a severe throat ailment and had gone to live with his Grandmother Goode in the Austrian Tyrol. There, the "little brown boy" was doted on by his governess and his grandmother. He had learned French and German quickly and next spent a year in school in Switzerland. Finally, Pauli had gone to Canada with his grandmother to attend school in Montreal.

When Paul and Essie returned to the United States, they wanted Pauli with them. They put him in school at home, where he stayed until Paul's tour and film chores were completed. The time went all too fast. Paul didn't have the heart to leave his son behind in the States while he and Essie returned to London, so he had young Pauli brought over to England in Mrs. Goode's charge.

And back in London, Paul had time to spend with his son. The boy was remarkable. He was an exact image of his father, only smaller and a bit lighter in complexion; and he could speak three languages with ease. The father had certainly missed his son, but he hadn't realized until now how much his son had missed. When Pauli had been allowed on the retake set of *Sanders of the River*, he had said, "Look! There are black people—lots of black people—just like us!"

It was Essie who saw at once what had to be done for Pauli. She would take her eight-year-old son to Africa with her. There was little chance now that Paul could accompany them. His work in motion pictures was gathering momentum, and as much as he would have liked to go, he could not leave London.

Essie and Pauli began their trip on May 29, 1936. All preparations had been made, their bags were packed and the day of the journey should have begun with light and promise. But the day turned out to be dismal and cold, with a grey sky full of foreboding. Paul wondered if he wasn't insane to let his wife and son go off alone into Africa. And with a heart heavy with sadness, he saw them onto the train and into their compartments for the first leg of their journey.

Pauli looked up at his father with his round eyes full of love. He couldn't have known how great the distance he would travel. He knew for sure only that again he must leave his father.

Paul leaned down to kiss Pauli, and then, Essie. The train eased out of the station. Alone on the platform, Paul stood stiff and silent in a state of mild shock. There never seemed time for him and Essie to be together with Pauli. He felt grief at having his son away from him again but he steeled himself and began working harder than ever.

Essie called him from Capetown, South Africa, and he was greatly relieved to hear her voice. Over the long distance, he managed to sound self-possessed. Essie was full of news and excitement. Pauli was fine, just fine. And she was keeping a journal. She intended to write down the highlights of her and Pauli's journey, from their southernmost point in Africa to their northern port of return, Cairo, Egypt.

After the call, Paul was reassured that his wife and son would be all right. And he began working long hours on the film *Song of Freedom*. The intricate plot of *Song of Freedom* involved a royal medallion once worn by Queen Zinga of Casanga Island. The medallion is traced through history, from Africa to America and on through the Civil War. In later times, it comes to light again, worn by a black American dock worker, John Zinga (played by Paul Robeson), who knows nothing about the history of the medallion.

Paul believed *Song of Freedom* to be an important film because it fused African with black American culture. For black Americans were not generally aware at this time of Africa's former greatness, nor that those who came here as slaves were descended from extraordinary peoples. And, indeed, when it was released, the *Pittsburgh Courier* called it "a story of triumph . . . the finest story of colored folks yet brought to the screen."[1]

The motion picture was shot at Beaconsfield (outside of London), and this time, Paul had some control over the script. In his contract he had the right to approve *Song of Freedom*'s final editing.

Meantime, he continued his study of languages and began reading another film script for his next movie. The picture was to be *King Solomon's Mines*, from the book by H. Rider Haggard. The story was about the adventures of Allan Quartermaine who travels to Zimbabwe in Southern Rhodesia to search for the mines of King Solomon. Paul was to portray Umbopas, Chief of the Mashona tribe, who helps Quartermaine in his search. Paul very much wanted to make Umbopas a man true to reality and not some "noble savage." And he hoped with this film, as he had hoped with *Song of Freedom*, to reverse the image of the shuffling, bug-eyed blacks shown in too many Hollywood movies.

At the end of August, Paul went to Paris to greet Essie and Pauli coming home from Africa. Paul was so glad to see them and they all had a wonderful reunion, with Pauli and Essie well and happy. Essie had her journal filled with notes, which she had often scribbled hastily as they traveled the continent of Africa by almost any means.

Early in September, Paul was busy filming *King Solomon's Mines*, with the star Sir Cedric Hardwicke playing Allan Quartermaine. But his dream for a true picture of Africa and an African were not to be realized in this film. Even though he had some control over the final editing, any worthwhile contribution to reality was defeated by the film's melodramatic style.

Never one to sit still for long, Paul carried on, still

hoping for the proper film to come along that would use his full talent of voice and acting ability. But he didn't wait for it. He was again in the Soviet Union by January 1937, where he gave concerts in Moscow and in the factories of the hinterland. He traveled east to Soviet Asia and to the Caucasus region, where he saw that the nonliterate peoples had very quickly reached a modern level of industrialization. Men who had been herdsmen now farmed with tractors. People who twenty years earlier had no written language were going to school, reading, writing and attending universities.

He was struck by the fact that all peoples, once given the chance, could take part in modern life. Africans, American blacks, Soviet Asians, were "backward" not because they were black, or yellow, but because they had never had the opportunity to learn. With this new thought in mind, he took a decisive step for his son, Pauli.

The New York Times reported, in a special cable from Moscow, on December 21, 1936:

> Paul Robeson, noted American Negro singer now making a concert tour of Russia, will place his 9-year-old son, Paul Jr., in school here instead of America so the boy need not contend with discrimination because of color until he is older and his father can be with him.

The story went on to say that "Mr. Robeson is immensely liked by the Russians. . . . He denied current rumors that he intends to become a Soviet citizen, saying America is his country."

Once Pauli had studied the Russian language, he would go to Moscow, but not until then.

Back in England a few months later, Paul began work on still another film production. This one was entitled *Jericho* and would be called *Dark Sands* when released in the United States. Paul was to play the part of Jericho Jackson, a black soldier on a torpedoed troop ship who is forced to shoot his black sergeant while attempting to save other black soldiers. Jericho Jackson is sentenced to death but escapes, and encounters a white soldier who is himself on the run. The two go to Africa where Jackson becomes the Chief of the Nomadic Tuareg tribe of North Africa. Eventually, he leads his tribe on a fantastic journey across the Sahara Desert.

For part of the filming, Paul had to go to Africa. It was his first trip and once there on that continent that had long stirred his dreams, he had expected the dreams to come to life. What he saw was Egypt, and although the people of Cairo were dark of skin, he saw nothing that could project for him the extraordinary beauty of black Africa nor the diversity of its tribes and peoples. He had somehow expected the very earth to be imbued with a unique black spirit, the same spirit he hoped would pervade the film *Jericho*.

He did not see *his* Africa at all, for the land of his ancestors was not so different from other places he had been. It was not special as he had so long believed it would be. The unique spirit of *his* Africa existed in his mind and in the minds of others like him who hoped for a free and independent Africa. The great continent was instead caught in the vise of colonialism, and governed and exploited by European countries. There were only two parts of black Africa still free. They were Ethiopia—formerly Abyssinia—and Liberia.

Italy, one of the exploiting countries, had long been dissatisfied with peace arrangements after the First World War. Italian forces had also been humiliated in a defeat by Abyssinia (Ethiopia) at Aduwa in 1896. Indeed, failure has a long memory. Italy went to war with Ethiopia in 1935 and ruthlessly conquered the country in 1936, despite the futile pleas for help by Ethiopian Emperor Haile Selassie to the League of Nations (the world organization of nations promoting peace).

And here began the certain rise of a new and rigid order never before known in the world, which did battle with freedom—in Africa, in Spain, in China and in Germany. Although it was given various political party names, such as Nazism in Germany, it is known generally as *totalitarianism*. It grew out of men's minds as a part of life just as freedom had.

Totalitarianism is a method of life and civilization opposed to all individual liberty. And yet, its appeal grew and spread.

Italian Premier Benito Mussolini believed he had found an alternative to capitalist democracy as well as communism. He despised both, saying that democracy split people into selfish minority parties and that communism was worthless, having been brought into being by capitalist society. The totalitarian regime which he devised in the 1930's he termed "Fascism." Fascism, Mussolini stated, was the "dictatorship of the State over many classes (employer and employee) co-operating."

By 1939, totalitarianism—Italian Fascism, German Nazism—spread throughout Europe. Only ten out of twenty-seven European countries remained democratic—that is, had various political parties competing for office. The Soviet Union still worked through the Marxist "dictatorship of the proletariat." All other European countries had regimes which were authoritarian or fascistic.

Paul Robeson returned to England from Africa knowing that the world was in the throes of oppression, and aware that he now thought first about the world and only then of himself. Where were freedom and equality—for the world, not just for himself? And where was peace—not only for himself? The great celebrity concerts he had once given to the upper and middle classes of England seemed pompous and futile now. For he had been transformed by his study of Marxism and his concern for oppressed Africans, Spaniards, Jews, into making a crucial change in his life.

He made up his mind to appear in public where ordinary working people could come and where they would pay no more than sixpence in admission. So it was that he began to sing in the English music halls and flashy movie theaters where tickets were cheap. Sometimes, he appeared as often as three times a day. And he worked with the Unity Theatre of the British labor movement. The Unity Theatre was a "people's theater," designed to dramatize the life of the workingman and the peace struggle, and to help in bringing about a better economic and social ideal. Unity did not want drama that provided escape from reality, but plays that showed modern life as it was lived by ordinary people.

Unity was the type of theater Paul had been looking for and now the money he made was hardly anything compared to the huge sums he had once made.

Critics began to say his voice was strained and harsh.

But Paul didn't really mind. What was important was that he was reaching a much wider audience and he was expressing his belief in the common bond between all those who labor.

"When I step on to a stage," he said, ". . . I go on as a representative of the working class."[2]

But he never talked very much about what he was doing and he didn't worry about the money he lost. He performed a benefit for besieged Ethiopia at the request of Emperor Haile Selassie's daughter. The concert also benefited nationalist China, whose mainland had been invaded by Japan. Paul asked no fee for himself. As he said, it was his pleasure to sing for freedom. And sing he did, in the various languages of the Soviet Union, in Hebrew, in Yiddish; he sang spirituals, too, and cante hondo, the blues of Spain. Paul sang for anyone, anywhere, for whatever cause he felt was just.

In the world at this time, the fight of all common people, white and black, had to be against the suppression of freedom and the rise of fascism. How long the races would work together was not a question that Paul worried about. But to his immense credit, as long as people needed him, he would work for the common good.

A year earlier, in February 1936, various political parties in Spain had aligned themselves with the democratic Spanish Republic established in 1931. Socialists, republicans, Anarchists and Communists all joined in a "Popular Front." The Popular Front won a strong victory in the elections, against the combined force of the former monarchy of Alfonso XIII, the ancient power of the Catholic Church, and the Spanish military. And it seemed that the government of the Spanish Republic was secure at last. But in July, an army general, Francisco Franco, led a Fascist insurrection against the government.

Spain quickly fell into civil war, and for nearly three years, Franco fought against the government. For the rest of the world, the Popular Front to fight fascism in Spain became the symbol of freedom. Ordinary men along with famous men left their countries to go to Spain and to fight for the Spanish Republic. There were the International Brigade, The American Volunteers and the Thälmann Brigade composed of freedom lovers fleeing from Nazi Germany, to name a few groups.

Britain's labor leaders called a mass meeting at Albert Hall at the time of the Christmas holiday in 1937. Paul and Essie attended. Labour statesman Clement Attlee told of his visit to Spain. Now he had returned to raise money for the republican armies fighting in the ongoing Spanish Civil War (1936-39).

Paul sang "Ol' Man River," changing the words in the first and second lines of the last verse from "Ah gits weary an' sick of tryin', Ah'm tired of livin' and skeered of dyin'," to "But I keeps laffin' instead of cryin', I must keep fightin' until I'm dyin'." The responsive roar of the audience was overwhelming. Here he was, creating new and vital folk music out of his own politics and beliefs.

Paul and Essie Robeson went to Barcelona, Spain,
where Paul sang for the International Brigade for Republican Spain. There, he saw Americans, Frenchmen,
Spaniards, non-Nazi Germans, antifascist Italians willing to give up their lives in a civil war that had become *their* personal war for liberty as well as
Spain's. Newspapers ran photographs of Paul standing
alone singing for hundreds of gun-toting troops. There
was another photograph of him wandering through
the barricaded streets of Madrid, his coat collar
turned up and his hands deep in his pockets.

The totalitarian governments of Germany and Italy
supplied planes for Franco's armies. Twenty-seven nations, including France, England and the U.S., agreed
not to intervene or take sides in the Spanish war.
Thus, because of an Allied nonintervention policy, the
Franco Fascists had the only air power in the war;
and they pounded the cities into rubble with their in-
discriminate bombing.

In Madrid, Paul sang amid actual bombing, surrounded by the horror of war. He went on from there
to France and to England, always singing, recruiting
for the international brigades and raising money for
the Spanish Republic. The common enemy was fascism, and the suffering of free Spain expressed the
suffering of oppressed peoples everywhere.

For him, the time passed swiftly. For several weeks,
he played the role of a union organizer in *Plant in the
Sun*, a short working-class play written by American
writer Ben Bengal and directed by Herbert Marshall.
He went on tour with Lawrence Brown, giving concerts for workers. Pauli Robeson, his study of Russian
now advanced, went off to Moscow with Essie's
mother and to school with the children of Communist
leaders.

Paul sang and sang for Republican Spain. The new
year, 1939, came, and the Spanish Civil War had split
the world into fascist and antifascist camps. In an extraordinary mass meeting in London held to welcome

home what was left of two British battalions, Paul sang militant labor songs of the world.

But the forces of Spanish fascist General Franco were winning. His army of 300,000 men struck at Barcelona and the poorly equipped army of the Republic could not stop it. Barcelona surrendered to Franco on January 26th. By the end of March 1939, Franco's victorious troops had entered Madrid, the capital of Spain. With the surrender of Madrid, Spain fell to Franco's Fascist political party, which abolished labor unions and forbade labor strikes. All workers were made to join nationally controlled syndicates and every industry was placed under the supervision of the Franco party syndicate.

General Franco became head of state in Spain and was called El Caudillo, The Leader. By August 1939, he had complete dictatorial authority over Spain and was, he said, "responsible only to God and to history."

The war which should have been a great cause for freedom ended with fascism triumphing in Spain. The American volunteers came home again, except for the ones who had died. They came home and, as Milton Wolf, the Commander of the American Volunteers in Spain, wrote in the *London Daily World*:

> They looked like everyone else—they had no uniforms and no one gave them any medals or ribbons . . . so that you could tell they had been at Madrid, or Teruel, or had crossed the Ebro. No Purple Hearts to go with the crutches, artificial limbs, empty sleeves, darkened eyes, or the wound in the heart that was a comrade dead. They were at home and they looked like everyone else but they were different and they would never be the same as anyone else again.

Millions of words such as the above were written to deplore the war. In less than a year of fighting, a thousand poems had been written. The great Spanish poet of the Republic, Federico Garcia Lorca, wrote a

ballad about the Spanish Civil Guard. He was killed
by them before one of Franco's firing squads, and
thrown into a hole.

> *Their horses are black.*
> *Black are their iron shoes.*
> *On their capes shimmer stains*
> *of ink and wax.*
> *They have, and so they never weep,*
> *skulls of lead.*
> *With patent-leather souls*
> *they come down the road. . . .*[3]

Paul Robeson, who had sung everywhere for the
Republic of Spain, was forty years old when the Spanish Civil War ended in 1939. Back in March, he had
pledged himself to aid the Republic by "adopting" a
hundred children of Spain. Between the ending of the
war and the time he had stood on the London stage to
sing "Ol' Man River" for the first time in 1928, the
years had accumulated like fallen leaves. They had
blown him suddenly to the threshold of middle age.
And there he had discovered his own true nature; he
could declare himself unhesitatingly on the side of
freedom everywhere and against oppression anywhere. Being an artist, he had learned to interpret
freedom and oppression through folk songs of the
world. Through his music, he was able to make different peoples realize they had the same needs, the same
fears. He never wanted people to think he was making
propaganda through his music. But when he sang
such favorites as "Go Down, Moses," audiences did
become emotionally involved. The "Pharaoh" Hitler
and the "Pharaoh" Franco wouldn't let the people go.
So the people tried to escape and the situation of
these refugees was a problem that free people
couldn't ignore. Such real human struggle hit free peoples over the world right in their hearts, Paul knew.

In May of 1939, he and Lawrence Brown made a
concert tour of Scandinavia. The tour turned out to be

an incredible experience, with each of his concerts in
Stockholm, Oslo, Copenhagen, resulting in a demon-
stration against Nazism and fascism. In Oslo, some ten
thousand people waited *outside* the concert hall, unable to get in. Tall, Nordic people fell on their knees
and kissed Paul's hand upon hearing him in concert. A
few years later, the Nazis would forbid the Norwe-
gians to listen to his records, because, they insisted,
his "voice" was dangerous.

In London again after the tour, Paul started work
on a motion picture entitled *Proud Valley*. He was to
play the part of an ordinary worker, a miner who
lived in the coal-mining Rhondda Valley of Wales. His
role was significant, he felt, because it spotlighted the
common man, whether his daily life of work took
place in Virginia, California or Southampton. Moreover, his role showed blacks working alongside whites
as equals and without racial strife. The Hollywood
motion picture industry back home would never have
made a picture in which Paul was cast as a miner first
and a singer and a black second. He knew this, and it
alone justified his making the picture.

Racial equality was the democratic ideal in 1939.
And enthusiastically, Paul and others of the cast of
Proud Valley went into the mining district of Wales
to shoot the film. They lived in the homes of miners
while the film was being made. And they used as ex-
tras the people of the mines near Mardy, a village in
the Rhondda Valley, and shot actual scenes from life.

He was proud of his work; the role had been completely satisfying. However, by the time *Proud Valley*
premiered at the Leicester Square Theatre in March
of 1940, practically on the eve of World War II, Paul
was home in America—for good.

He had been self-exiled in many lands for longer
than he cared to think about. When he allowed himself, he would admit that he was even more than
slightly homesick for his country. Furthermore, he
could no longer ignore the situation in Europe—the
rise of fascism and the ominous talk of world war—or

the continuing difficulties facing his people back home. He and Essie left England; and at home, the America they found was not unpleasant. Times had changed; not a great deal, perhaps, but change for the better was in the air.

During the years of the Depression and President Franklin D. Roosevelt's administration, a powerful focus had been placed on the concept of racial equality. Blacks were not only receiving relief and money, but were actually working, thousands for the first time in years. They worked in the forests of America for the Civilian Conservation Corps (CCC). They built schools, bridges and roads for the Works Progress Administration (WPA). These public projects for those who needed work guaranteed blacks a living wage. The WPA gave work to black actors, artists and musicians also, in their various fields. Under government grants, black scholars were at last able to research and publish segments of black history.

Black reporters were invited to press conferences at the White House. The president's wife, Eleanor Roosevelt, made it a point to invite black children to visit her. Such simple decency made white America sit up and take notice.

Nevertheless, Paul Robeson experienced a racial insult almost on the day of his return. He had been invited as guest of honor to a tea at one of New York's finest hotels. When he strode toward the elevator, he was told he must go around to the freight elevator.

"Several years back," he said in an interview, "I would have smarted at this insult and carried the hurt for a long time. Now—no—I was just amused and explained to the elevator boy that I didn't belong with the freight, that, as I was the guest of honor at the tea my hosts might be surprised to see me arrive with the supplies."[4]

With that, he had continued on his way on the passenger elevator.

Perhaps America had not changed so much as had Paul's (and thousands of other blacks') reaction to it.

He hadn't turned on his heel at the insult from the elevator operator, but had been amused and undaunted. The slur to his manhood, his blackness, had not stopped him for a moment. Times and black people had changed. And the change had also come over the most renowned black man the world had ever known.

One reason for the Robesons' return to America in September 1939 was that Paul was to play the huge black worker in *John Henry*, a rather imperfect drama slated for a Broadway opening in January 1940. Rehearsals were to begin early in October 1939; Paul and Essie initially planned to stay in the United States for only a few months. But it was so good being home, they decided to stay. They took an apartment at 555 Edgecombe Avenue, with a spectacular view of the Harlem River. Pauli came back home, also, accompanied by Essie's mother, and was placed in the Ethical Culture School.

The press repeatedly questioned Paul about why he would now live in America.

Well, things had changed, Paul told them. The social reforms of the New Deal program of President Roosevelt had convinced him that at last there was someone in the White House who understood what it meant to be black.

Living in many countries, Paul explained, traveling, giving concerts, he'd learned that blacks were not the only oppressed peoples in the world. The Spanish Civil War had shocked the world and had brought to light the oppression of the Spanish worker. He had kept close contact with the working class of England. And he knew the heartache of Jewish refugees from the Nazi nightmare. When he had sung black American folk songs, all of these peoples and others, too, had cried out in response. They had been deeply touched as if the music were theirs.

As an envoy for oppressed peoples, Paul had come home. His return to the American concert stage would prove successful over the next seven years and his popularity would remain high. He would crisscross the country singing to aid the war effort. His list of concert songs broadened geographically as well as politically—more Russian songs, more English; the American George Gershwin's "I Got Plenty of Nothin'" and "It Ain't Necessarily So"; the Spanish republican song "Los Quatros Generales," which Paul sang with such inspiring strength and sincerity that his audiences would begin to weep. As always, he refused to sing ever before a segregated audience.

Soon after Paul's return, the Columbia Broadcasting System began a new Sunday afternoon radio program entitled *The Pursuit of Happiness,* with Burgess Meredith as Master of Ceremonies. Its young radio producer, Norman Corwin, had come across a patriotic poem written by John Latouche and set to music by Earl Robinson. Corwin dusted off the piece and called it "Ballad for Americans." He thought he might use it on CBS's *Pursuit of Happiness* program and managed to get Paul to sing it.

The radio audience, which was fond of listening to symphony music on Sunday, was pleased when the announcement came that Mr. Robeson, recently returned to America, would now sing. The audience leaned back comfortably; then sat stunned as, for eleven minutes, Paul sang in his extraordinary baritone, with Earl Robinson's American People's Chorus strong and steady behind him:

> *Man in white skin can never be free*
> *While his black brother is in slavery.* . . .
>
> *Our country's strong, our country's young*
> *And her greatest songs are still unsung.*
> *From her plains and mountains we have sprung.* . . .
>
> *Out of the cheating, out of the shouting,*
> *Out of the murders and lynching,*

Out of the windbags, the patriotic spouting,
Out of uncertainty and doubting
Out of the carpet bag and the brass spittoon,
It will come again.
Our marching song will come again.
Simple as a hit tune, deep as our valleys
High as our mountains, strong as the people
who made it.[1]

Six hundred people in the studio audience shouted their pleasure and stamped their feet after Paul had finished. *Time* magazine reported that the audience thundered with applause "for two minutes while the show was still on the air, for fifteen minutes after."

> In the next half-hour [*Time* continued] 150 telephone calls managed to get through CBS's jammed Manhattan switchboard. The Hollywood switchboard was jammed for two hours. In the next few days bales of letters demanded words, music, recordings, another time at bat for "Ballad for Americans."

"Ballad for Americans" was no ordinary song of patriotism, for it expressed faith in *all* of the people. And overnight, it became the most popular song in the country:

> *"Who are you? . . ."*
> *Well, I'm the everybody who's nobody.*
> *I'm the nobody who's everybody.*
> *"Are you an American?"*
> *Am I an American?*
> *I'm just an Irish, Negro, Jewish, Italian,*
> *French, and English, Spanish, Russian,*
> *Chinese, Polish, Scotch, Hungarian,*
> *Litvak, Swedish, Finnish, Canadian,*
> *Greek and Turk, and Czech*
> *and double-Czech American. . . .*

* * *

It had been sung by the right kind of man, a black man, Paul Robeson, the symbol of oppression overcoming forces of darkness and doom. And finally, it was the perfect hit song to come along at the right time. For the Roosevelt Administration had rid itself of neutrality and was now able to help its allies threatened by Hitler's announced aim to take over Europe. So it was that the country needed a unified self-image, and the simple tune "Ballad for Americans" gave it confidence.

"Ballad for Americans" was sung again and again, in concert, at political rallies, on records, by amateur groups, by everyone. The American People's Chorus sang it 113 times in two and a half years. Paul recorded it for Victor Records. If all Americans had not known him before, they certainly knew him now, from the hinterland of the Middle West and Northwest to the great cities throughout the country. He experienced immense love and popularity from his countrymen, the first black American ever to be thus flattered. The press eagerly sought him out, demanding his comments on a wide range of subjects.

What did he think about Russia, the press wanted to know? What did he think about Germany?

The Second World War began in 1939 with the German invasion of Poland. With more than a million men, and with armored divisions and the massive air power of the Luftwaffe (the German air force), Hitler's Germany overran western Poland and within a month had added it to the Third Reich. Acting under secret clauses of the Hitler-Stalin Non-Aggression Pact, the Soviets two weeks laster assaulted the eastern half of Poland. By making the Soviets allies on its eastern border, Germany was assured it would not have to fight in the east and west at the same time. The pact with Germany, moreover, gave the Soviet Union time to build up its own military strength. When this secret union of German Nazism and Soviet Communism became known, it stupefied the world and bitterly disillusioned Americans sympathetic to the Soviets.

Furthermore, the USSR set up military bases in the Baltic states of Estonia, Latvia and Lithuania. Finland alone refused to give the Soviets military rights within their country or to give them rights to their border territories. However, the second major Soviet city, Leningrad, lay just twenty miles from the Finnish border; the Soviets insisted on territories surrounding it. The Finns refused, and in November 1939, the Soviet Union attacked this small neighboring country. By March 1940, the fighting was over. Finland had been forced to give up territory and the Soviet Union created a new Soviet republic out of Finnish lands.

With the Soviet attack on Finland, people of the Western democracies became furious. The British and French sent supplies and equipment to Finland, and the USSR was expelled from the League of Nations. But alone and in secret, the Soviet Union prepared for the battle it knew it would eventually have to wage against Hitler's Third Reich. The Western world, familiar with ideological differences, was not used to the power politics of the Hitler-Stalin Pact. But the Soviet Union had turned away from the British and French after having tried during the summer of 1939 to form with them an anti-German alliance. The USSR felt that what the French and British really wanted was for the Union to take the brunt of any Nazi attack. And so, instead, it signed a treaty of nonagression and friendship with Germany.

With the rise of fascist dictators in about 1935, liberal forces in the United States had supported the communist position of a "Popular Front." At this time the Comintern became officially inactive as all Communist parties in every country joined socialists and advanced liberals to fight fascism. But after the attack on Finland, American liberals felt betrayed.

Paul Robeson was asked what he thought about the Soviet attack; as a prominent liberal he couldn't refuse to comment. He had always spoken what he felt was the truth. Now, he questioned reports that Russia had attacked Finland. How could he be certain that the newspaper reports were true, when he knew from his own experience that the press could at times be untrustworthy? If the reports were true, then Finland must have done something. He had seen Soviet citizens fighting fascists in Barcelona and Madrid and he would not believe that the USSR was turning toward fascism itself. The truth had to have been distorted in some way by irresponsible newsmen.

The distortion was the fact that a complicated situation had been portrayed in simplistic terms. The Soviet Union had, indeed, attacked Finland, not in a simple assault but, lacking allies against Germany, as a political move of self-protection. However, this was the first instance that Paul's point of view separated him from "liberal" America—socialists, "left-wing" factions, and blacks. It would not be the last.

The Herbert Hoover Relief Fund for Finnish civilians sought to raise money for oppressed Finns by presenting a theatrical benefit in New York. The time was the end of January 1940. The Fund wanted Paul for the benefit; he refused.

For the first time, the American press became unfriendly toward him. It implied that Paul Robeson, made in America, owing all of his triumphs to his country, was turning away from the land of his birth.

"Robeson," said the Associated Press, "who has lived in England for the last ten years, . . . whose son was educated in Moscow, said he was not personally a Communist. . . ."[2]

The question of communism had never come up before in relation to Paul. One could sympathize with the Soviet Union without being a communist. Many had and still did. The issue had been raised now because of the extraordinary feeling against the Soviets for attacking Finland. It would be raised again and again.

Nevertheless, the Finnish relief incident faded from memory. If people remembered Paul Robeson in relation to it, then they saw it as an isolated failure in the life of an incredibly busy, popular and gifted man and thought no more about it. Yet a certain change had come over Paul. He seemed more serious and less willing to smile so easily. Troubles in Europe, in the world and in his own country seemed to weigh heavily upon him. Wherever he went, he was besieged by reporters and adoring fans, and forced into some public stance. But within himself, he was, perhaps, more alone than ever. And seeing an acquaintance in a crowd, he would greet him like a long-lost friend.

Early in January, Paul had opened on Broadway in *John Henry*, which apparently had no theatrical magic. Critics called it uneven, although they said Paul was magnificent, a man who should be seen much more and in plays worthy of his talent.

Only five performances of *John Henry* were given before the play closed and, according to the New York *Amsterdam News*, it lost almost $100,000. But the drama's failure did not stop Paul's forward thrust into American society, nor the impression he made. He went on tour with Lawrence Brown. He sang at southern black colleges, where school administrators would admit whites and blacks together to hear him.

His audiences grew ever larger when on June 23, 1941, the largest audience of all came out to hear him sing "Ballad for Americans"—13,000 people at New York's Lewisohn Stadium. Tall, dark and superbly at ease in the spotlight, he was near the peak of his fame. More than ever now, he stood out before the public, impressing it and influencing it with his artistry. Yet he hoped to help his own people most by associating his good name with large labor unions and workers' organizations.

The day before Paul's Lewisohn Stadium triumph, an event for which the Soviet Union had made secret preparation took place. On June 22nd, Germany broke its pact with the Union. And in one of the most incredible mistakes Hitler ever made, he invaded the vast Soviet Union, pouring in three million troops along a two-thousand-mile front. Although the Soviets would win in the siege of Stalingrad in 1943, they would lose more men in this one battle than the United States would lose in the whole war.

Now France, which had already fallen to Germany, and England, at war with Germany, had an ally, the Soviet Union, who could pin down the German army on the eastern front. On June 24, President Roosevelt announced that war supplies would be lent or leased to the new ally. Although not yet at war, the United States also proceeded to adopt the draft and build up its army, air force and navy. It made plans to defend the Americas with the help of Latin American republics; and it secured its bases in Iceland and Greenland.

With the Nazi invasion of the Soviet Union, the war in Europe took on a tone of more deadly seriousness and there was great sympathy in America for the Soviets.

Paul Robeson's pro-Russian attitude no longer seemed odd or strange. He and Essie were considered people knowledgeable about the Soviet Union. Paul's long interest in all things Russian and his understanding of the Russian language was one of the reasons he now became a sought-after speaker. He joined organizations such as the Joint Anti-Fascist Refugee Committee, the Committee to Aid China and the Council on African Affairs, of which he became Chairman.

Soon, he and Essie decided to move out of New York into the country, for Paul needed a retreat away from his professional obligations. Pauli was placed in the Technical High School at Springfield, Massachusetts, and Essie found a big rambling house set in two and one half acres of land in Enfield, Connecticut. They bought the house to give privacy to Paul and also to give space to Pauli's energy. The estate, called "The Beeches," was a place they came to love, even though Paul was never quite at ease with its swimming pool, tennis court and billiard room. Essie felt that now she could continue her studies in anthropology, and enrolled in the Hartford Seminary to work for her Ph.D.

In July, Paul was made an honorary member of the National Maritime Union at its convention held in Cleveland, Ohio. The NMU had a large black membership and was one of the most militant unions in America. At the convention, Paul sang ten songs and spoke briefly, saying he was "awfully happy and optimistic because fascism has at last come to grips with the one power that will show it no quarter" (the USSR). Then, he urged the United States to give all possible aid to the Soviet Union—which it did, with quantities of armaments two years later in the siege of Stalingrad.

Often now, Paul found himself aligned with civil-liberties leaders, the so-called left wing, in his public life. In September 1941, he worked with the Citizens Committee to Free Earl Browder, who was head of the American Communist Party. Mr. Browder had been jailed because of his antiwar activities; and in his behalf, Paul made a brief speech and sang at Madison Square Garden before a crowd of 20,000.

In October, German submarines sank an American destroyer. And on December 7, 1941, Japanese air and naval forces attacked the U.S. fleet at Pearl Harbor naval bases in Hawaii and in the Philippines, Guam and Midway Islands. The next day, the U.S. Congress declared war on Japan. On December 11, Germany and Italy declared war on the United States, which then declared a state of war with them.

With the Japanese attack on Pearl Harbor, the American naval force in the Pacific was devastated and the United States was pulled headlong into World War II. The war brought the communist USSR and the capitalist USA much more closely together on the same side of battle. Furthermore, good race relations at home became essential to national unity. Racism was no longer a respectable public position, at least not in the North. Publishers of magazines, books and periodicals began representing black life and history with much more accuracy.

Earlier in the year, President Roosevelt, under pressure from black leaders, had issued an order protecting the rights of black Americans. The order was the first of its kind since the Emancipation Proclamation—Order #8802 banning discrimination in all factories or plants that were working on national defense contracts. As in the past when the life of the nation was at stake, blacks were allowed some measure of freedom and equality. Yet it is significant that President Roosevelt did not extend his executive order to ban discrimination in the armed forces. Black men were segregated completely in the army and in other branches of the service into all-black fighting forces. At home, black workers were integrated for the purpose of arms production.

Violations of the civil rights of black people continued, however, and were part of the reason Paul donated his services in the production of a documentary film entitled *Native Land,* produced by Frontier Films. Essentially plotless, the film's subject was America's internal fight for freedom against oppression and vigilante groups such as the Ku Klux Klan. Paul spoke the commentary for this film based on a Senate investigation of discrimination in the Southern states. He also sang the musical score.

A year later, in the autumn of 1942, Congressman Martin Dies, Democrat from Texas and Chairman of the House Un-American Activities Committee, presented to Congress a list of names of people and organizations he considered "anti-American." Those on the list, he stated, were communists, and on the list was the name of Paul Robeson, and the film organization Frontier Films.

Martin Dies accused the Robert Marshall Foundation of giving Frontier Films six thousand dollars to produce "the communist film *Native Land.*" The foundation often gave money to organizations which aided race relations in Southern states. Martin Dies further stated, erroneously, that the film was based on the book *Native Son,* by the black novelist Richard Wright. He stated that Mr. Wright and Mr. Robeson were also members of what he called a "front" organization for the Communist Party.

Congressman Dies was the first man to accuse Paul, by implication, of being a Communist. But in 1942, such charges as "Communist" and such vague notions as "guilt by association" were not very serious for Paul. For the political climate in America was not strongly anti-Communist, since the USSR, the greatest Communist power the world had known, was a close ally. Moreover, the Dies committee only represented a vocal minority and had little effect on the renowned Robeson, who freely gave his all to the war effort, and who appeared at war-bond rallies and war plants for the government.

Over and over again, the nation was being told that it and its allies were waging a war to free humanity of the worst tyrants the world had known. If we won this war, then democracy and freedom would be ours forever.

Paul Robeson believed that when the war was over and peace had come, he and his black people would live in a truly democratic America. Racial equality would be a fact of his life and black lives for generations to come.

And so Paul sang. Traveling north and south, he sang for freedom before huge audiences—30,000 in Hollywood, 150,000 in Chicago. He sang at San Quentin Prison and New York's Carnegie Hall. He seemed taller, blacker, stronger, his superb baritone better than ever.

Yet in his travels, he was made to sit in segregated cars of trains, in separate dining areas; he had to use segregated train-station waiting rooms and washrooms as did all blacks. He had to accept these Jim Crow conditions if he ever hoped to reach blacks across the country. But the acceptance rankled, for what was called democracy allowed two systems to exist—the one that praised and rewarded him as an artist and the other which discriminated against him as a black man.

After the war, the two systems would have to end. For black soldiers, fighting to insure democracy in Europe, could not possibly be denied it when they returned home. So Paul believed throughout the war years.

His dedicated work for freedom was deeply appreciated by black people and he received an honorary Doctor of Humane Letters from Morehouse College, the black school in Atlanta, Georgia. The award from Morehouse was the first he had received from his own people. It made him so very happy and proud, also.

During the years of World War II, Paul made hundreds of records and lent his deep, stirring voice to as many concerts. In order to save his voice from strain, he began using microphones for singing in large concert halls and outdoor stadiums. The microphone and an "acoustical device" which helped him hear himself as he sang received considerable comment from the press. Some reviewers felt that voice amplification was improper and unnatural. Nevertheless, Paul used the microphone from 1940 on, and with increasing acceptance from the public. As often as he could, he went to his home—the Beeches—in Connecticut to rest. He had never had long periods just for relaxation; and he had even less time now. For one of the major directors in American theater, Margaret Webster, decided to stage *Othello* for Broadway with Paul playing the lead.

The year was 1942 and Miss Webster had a difficult time casting the role of Iago, Othello's traitorous friend, and Desdemona, Othello's wife. White actors and actresses were afraid that American audiences would never sit for a play such as *Othello,* which showed a black man in a love scene with a white woman. But finally, Miss Webster was able to cast two young and not very well-known actors as Iago and Desdemona. They were José Ferrer, a Puerto Rican, and his wife, Uta Hagen. Miss Webster's plan was to take *Othello* into summer stock. If she found audiences could accept Paul as Othello the Moor playing opposite white Desdemona, she could be assured of some success when she brought the production to Broadway at the end of October 1943.

Paul was thrilled to be acting the Othello role again. Here he was, almost forty-five years old. And yet, he looked much the same as he had ten years before, when he had played Othello in London. Now, he knew he had matured and he would play Othello as never before.

Then came months of hard, exacting work putting the *Othello* production into shape. In August, it was tried out in Cambridge, Massachusetts, and again in Princeton, Paul's hometown. There had been no racial incidents in either city. Reviews had been more than favorable, as in the one in *Time* magazine on August 24, 1942:

> On the tiny stage of a straw-hat theater in Cambridge, Mass., last week Paul Robeson made his first U.S. appearance in *Othello*. After seeing him, scholars might still insist that Shakespeare meant Othello for a Moor and not a Negro. But drama lovers well might ask why, having played it twelve years ago in London, Robeson waited so long to play it over here. For in spite of muffing certain speeches—his lines sometimes throbbed awkwardly—and overacting certain scenes—his Grand Manner sometimes burst a seam—Robeson gave a performance that even at it worst was vivid and that at its best was shattering.

Paul had not gone into the Broadway production thinking it would be the ultimate success or failure of his life. He was more interested in showing his countrymen that Shakespeare, perhaps the greatest of all playwrights, had written a timeless tragedy about a black general trying to cope with a white Renaissance world.

When the producers, The Theatre Guild, announced that the production would open on Broadway on October 19, 1943, the New York theater crowd went

slightly insane. Everyone had to see the play—and not
only the rich, who usually attended first nights. The
Shubert Theatre was sold out a week after the Guild's
announcement. Tickets were bought by theater buffs
and housewives, by housepainters as well as "stockmarket dukes" and "black-market barons." Soldiers
and sailors attended, as did professors and students;
actors and authors; musicians and painters, Hindus
and Europeans. And blacks. The people of Harlem
turned out eagerly for the opening.

And what a night! *Othello* was a superb production
full of pageantry in which Paul Robeson made no un-
necessary move, yet dominated the whole by his massive and intense calm.

José Ferrer as Iago proved his ability on the stage,
with a performance that was a perfect foil for Paul's
solemn quiet during the early part of the play. Ferrer
was all movement and all over the stage at once, so
that the contrast between his activity and Paul's sculp-
tured stillness was startling.

Time magazine said that Paul "was not so much
Othello as a great and terrible presence." For the
black press and the black community, he was their
finest, grandest name:

> More than any other American unless it be Roose-
> velt himself, he [Paul] typifies the individual
> whose world outlook contains a sympathetic un-
> derstanding of the commonness of every nation,
> race and time.[1]

Whether he had intended it to be or not, *Othello*
had become Paul's greatest triumph. The Shubert
Theatre echoed the applause for twenty minutes after
the last scene. And the production ran for two
hundred and ninety-six performances, the longest run
on Broadway for any Shakespeare play. It closed on
July 1, 1944, with the Guild's announcement:

* * *

Termination of the New York run is made necessary because of the heavy burdens of the leading role. If the rest of the country is to get the fresh performances to which it is entitled, a rest is imperative.

The whole of America was going to have a chance to see Paul play Othello. He would tour the country for fifteen hundred dollars a week, a fraction of what he could make playing a concert for one night.

The time that *Othello* ran on Broadway marked the period of Paul's undisputed fame in the United States. He was the most successful spokesman for Negro rights that blacks had at this time:

Negroes [he said] know that their rights can only be achieved in an America which has realized all of its democratic ideals. They know that their own struggle is bound up with the struggle against anti-Semitism and against injustices to all minority groups. They know that those sections of organized labor which have enlisted membership on a plane of strict equality constitute the Negro people's chief allies in the struggle for democratic rights, and they know, too, that the winning of the war against Fascism is the first and fundamental requirement toward the realization of a democratic America.[2]

And well aware that he was the people's "voice," Paul accepted the responsibility with pride:

The American Negro has changed his temper. Now he wants his freedom. Whether he is smiling at you or not, he wants his freedom. The old exploitation of peoples is definitely past.[3]

Everywhere he went, he was greeted by thousands of people of all races who looked on him as something close to a god. He won the American Academy of Arts and Sciences Gold Medal award for the best diction in the American theater and the Donaldson Award for the best acting performance in 1944, both for his *Othello* role. Appearing with Vice-President of the United States Henry Wallace, he lent himself to government causes and showed that the war effort was a national priority. Always, he made certain his country understood it could not have black patriotism only in time of crisis and then ignore that patriotism when the crisis had passed. Black patriotism would be everlasting, he said, as long as America gave blacks freedom in return.

Most of this time, Paul was traveling. He had few periods for rest in New York or even at The Beeches in Connecticut. When he was not appearing at political or defense meetings, he was giving America a taste of *Othello*. The road company of *Othello* began its tour in the autumn of 1944. It traveled to forty-five cities, ending in Chicago on April 10, 1945.

Today, across America, there are people who still remember the experience of seeing Paul as Othello. People in their mid-forties remember as high school students the extraordinary moment. Their eyes turn inward, going back in time, and they speak about it as though it happened only yesterday. Typical is the response of a white woman in southern Ohio:

> You have to understand, he was the first one I'd ever seen. I mean, I knew there were Negroes but I never *thought* about them. He was the first one I'd ever *seen*.

Indeed, for many he was the first, for he opened blind eyes to what blacks had to offer. White students, locked in their segregated neighborhoods as blacks were locked in theirs, saw for the first time a black giant. He was tall, so tall that he was a dark god whose voice made them tremble.

Blacks, too, remember his impact. "There's no way I

can tell you how I felt about him," a black taxi driver said. "It wasn't just because he was Paul Robeson. He was up there on that stage. . . . I'd never seen a stage before. . . . Big and as black as he could be, with that voice rolling out . . . like God! He was one of us. He was ours."[4]

In the theaters of America, students cried and moaned at the inevitable tragedy of Othello. When doom struck him, they rose from their seats, screaming and applauding and shouting for Robeson.

Backstage, he was as straight and tall as he had ever been. He wore the beard he had grown for *Othello* with perfect grace. Yet there were lines now, on his forehead, on his face, the only evidence that time had touched him. His shoulders did not sag; he held his head as proudly as ever. And when he smiled, he seemed to grow before one's eyes.

During the whole period of Paul's triumph, World War II had raged on and on. In the early stages of the war, the cause of freedom for which Paul had fought so hard seemed all but lost, for the Axis Powers— Germany, Italy and Japan—dealt powerful blows against the nations that held ideals of democracy. Italy had mounted an offensive in North Africa; Germany had invaded Russia and the Japanese conquered the Philippines, Malaya and the Dutch East Indies. They had swept into the Aleutian Islands, occupied Burma and were about to invade India. In the Atlantic, German submarines were sinking Allied ships nearly to the shores of the United States.

The Axis Powers were met and finally stopped only when Britain, the United States, the USSR and twenty-six smaller nations joined together as the Allied Powers. Each of these nations pledged never to make a separate peace and to use all of its resources to win against the Axis.

The United States and Britain coordinated their military power in a command called the Combined Chiefs of Staff. The Chiefs of Staff decided that Germany was the most formidable enemy and that the first effort would be made to defeat Hitler. It took America two years to mobilize for war, and not until 1944 did a complete Allied offensive take place.

On June 6, 1944, D-Day, the Allied invasion of Europe began. The time was dawn, the place was directly across the Channel from England on the coast of German-occupied France. An incredible force of American, Canadian and British troops with land, sea and air power and with gigantic tonnages of supplies assembled in England under the command of General Dwight D. Eisenhower. On the first day, over 100,000 men invaded the French coast of Normandy, and with tremendous casualties, established a beachhead. By the end of the month, a million men were on the coast and moving inland. By August, Paris was liberated of German occupation and in late January, Eisenhower's armed forces had crossed into Germany.

In the winter of 1942–43, the USSR had finally devastated part of the German army in the siege of Stalingrad. Then, early in 1945, the Soviet Army swept west into East Prussia, Hungary and Czechoslovakia. The Soviets began their final drive into Germany and were soon at the gates of Berlin. There they coordinated with American, British and Free French forces. It was agreed that a Soviet force would take Berlin. Hitler died in the ruins of the capital of his Third Reich. By May 8, 1945, the war in Europe was over.

On September 2, 1945, the Japanese surrendered unconditionally after atomic bombs were dropped by the United States over the cities of Hiroshima and Nagasaki, Japan.

World War II was at an end, with thirty million military and civilian deaths as the unalterable fact of its devastation, not including the six to ten million Jews and other ethnic and political minorities exterminated by Adolph Hitler. Such enormous loss of life staggers the mind. On the face of it, it would make little sense to say that peace had come.

Yet, that is what men said. Peace had come. And during the war, Allied leaders had said that freedom and equality would be at once forthcoming at the moment of peace. Franklin D. Roosevelt and Winston Churchill had issued the Atlantic Charter earlier, during the war, on August 14, 1941. The Charter pledged these "common principles," among others: the renunciation of territorial expansion; the restoration of self-government to those deprived of it; equal access to trade and raw materials to all peoples. The Four Freedoms—freedom of speech, freedom of religion, freedom from want and freedom from fear—enunciated earlier by President Roosevelt were incorporated into the Charter.

Allied governments had made the Charter commitment when they sought the aid of the world's colored and colonized peoples to fight fascism. Thus, colonized peoples—Indians, Africans and others—expected the Allies to establish free governments after the war. In the United States, black leaders such as Paul Robeson, Walter White and W.E.B. Du Bois wanted nothing less than full equality for American blacks.

But with the war's end a grim reality soon hit the world of colonized peoples. America and the USSR set up military governments in Korea, paying little attention to that country's people, who had been colonized by the Japanese for half a century.

There had been a native government in the Dutch East Indies when the Japanese withdrew, but now the British came in and established a colony once again. In the Philippines, America took over the government. In Indochina, the French re-established colonial rule. The USSR, in the sweep of military operations at the war's end, set up People's Republics in Eastern and Central Europe.

The war in Europe was over but separate political moves by the once Allied nations had begun immediately. The United States had reached a stage of imperialism at a period when exploited countries would no longer allow themselves to be ruled by whites or anyone else. Generally, America saw the third world as an economic source of labor and raw materials, or as sites for military bases. If and when the U.S. attempted to better conditions for third world peoples, her largess was usually regarded with suspicion:

> Americans who wanted to bring the blessings of democracy, capitalism, and stability to everyone meant just what they said—the whole world, in their view, should be a reflection of the United States. . . . The idea that the Third World would resent, and eventually struggle against, American domination was hardly considered.[5]

Even if America hadn't needed foreign markets, hostilities between the U.S. and the USSR would have created a race for weapons. Each time one nation developed a new weapon, the other found ways of defending itself by building a better weapon. Thus, there began an undeclared "Cold War" between these two great powers, the only two countries left standing strong after the end of World War II. What one did to protect itself, the other saw as an act of aggression. Smaller countries found it necessary to be *for* the USSR and *against* America or vice versa. It was no longer possible for other nations to be for both powerful countries, whose systems of economics and government were so vastly different.

Slowly, the world became two separate camps—cut in two by this Cold War of suspicion, fear and shrill political mouthings.

"From Stettin in the Baltic to Trieste in the Adriatic," said Sir Winston Churchill, "an iron curtain has descended across the continent [of Europe]."[6]

The "Iron Curtain" was said to have descended between the Soviet Union and the rest of the world. In a matter of months, the United States had given in to its historical fear of communism. And the USSR was no longer viewed as an ally, but as a great, brooding bear bent on destroying democracy and capitalism; so the United States believed.

The Allied world of unity seemed to be at an end.

President Franklin D. Roosevelt had died on April 12, 1945 (shortly before the end of the war), two days after Paul Robeson opened in the final run of *Othello* in Chicago. In the streets of America, people stood stunned, crying at the news of Roosevelt's death. Vice-President Harry S Truman had become President.

Paul Robeson publicly read a tribute to Roosevelt written by poet Carl Sandburg at a meeting of the Independent Citizens' Committee of the Arts, Sciences and Professions:

> *The art of the man is still now,*
> *Yet his shadow lingers alive and speaking*
> *To the whole family of man round the earth.*
> *His teaching ran that all nations must be neighbors;*
> *That their only choice is whether they shall be*
> *good neighbors or bad.*
> *He was a builder with genius for the solidarity*
> *of mankind*
> *In his own country and everywhere in other countries.*
> *Tokens and emblems and flowers we throw*
> *upon his coffin.*[7]

Victory in Europe was declared on the day that Paul's Chicago friends were giving a party for him. The party thus became doubly important. He was being honored, and in turn he and his friends gave thanks to peace and a happier world. He had kept the faith: all men were equal, and he would continue to work for the equality of all. At his party, with victory in Europe at hand, it seemed that the terrible war had brought people together in building a world of brotherhood. President Roosevelt was dead, it was true; but the Nazi Reich was smashed and Hitler had died with it. Paul dared to hope that a new era of goodwill and understanding had begun.

He and Lawrence Brown, with violinist Miriam Solovieff, rushed off to Europe in August of 1945, to entertain American troops still occupying war-torn countries. According to the press, they were the first interracial USO (United Service Organization) sponsored group to go overseas. Well-received, they gave twenty-five concerts, five a week for five weeks.

Paul came home only to find that Americans appeared to want to return to "normalcy," to conditions as they had been before the war. The sentiment was that good old prewar America was good enough. Many broad-minded people like him had hoped that by 1946, the U.S. would place itself on the side of liberal thought at home and in Europe, Asia and Africa. But the Roosevelt liberalism was falling away in the sweep of conservative and reactionary elements in this country and overseas. Social progress, change, became increasingly suspect as subversive.

Paul thought it disgraceful that World War II veterans came back to America to find there were not enough jobs to go around and not enough homes. Black veterans not only faced these problems, but more racial discrimination, which they had been told they had fought to destroy. Although progress had been made in legal civil rights, practical opposition to black advancement was well entrenched. Paul was deeply angered and shaken by this reaction to progress.

Still, he had come home after the tour as the black envoy and the embodiment of the American dream. He was as popular as ever, if not more so. The National Association for the Advancement of Colored People gave him its Spingarn Medal in the autumn of 1945. It was the highest honor given each year to a black man.

During the war years, Paul had confined his politics largely to the kinds of songs he sang. As Cold War tensions increased, many did not look favorably on his singing of Russian songs. Furthermore, Paul began to speak out politically.

Soon after receiving the Spingarn Medal, he spoke before one of the most important Jewish groups in the country, the Central Conference of American Rabbis. Rabbis and Jewish laymen from Eastern and Midwestern states had come together to discuss the "relationship of the teaching of Judaism to race problems confronting the world."[8]

The rabbis could not have chosen a more knowledgeable speaker. For Paul understood as few Americans did at this time that America was now creating her own empire. Widely traveled, well-read and deeply aware of any injustice, he knew that American soldiers, politicians and businessmen had expanded into Europe, Southeast Asia, Latin America and almost everywhere else. The military hunted overseas bases while politicians searched for areas such as the Dominican Republic, where their influence could dominate the government.

But what he told the rabbis and laymen shocked them as it did others reading the account in *The New York Times* the next day. Paul said that the United States "has taken over the role of Hitler," and now "stands for counter-revolution all over the world."[8]

He said that the secrets of the atomic bomb should be given to the USSR because "a strong Soviet Union would be the greatest guarantee against another world war." His black people might well chance dictatorship, which possibly could guarantee their rights, instead of depending on worn-out, often hollow promises of "freedom of speech."[8]

The rabbis and laymen were stunned at Paul's criticism of America, perhaps not comprehending the irony of his words about dictatorship. They had expected him to speak out. Yet they could not accept from a black man what thoughtful whites had been saying for quite some time: America was an imperialist power with a peculiarly "American dilemma." No one wanted to hear Paul Robeson say that his country wasn't the greatest democracy the world had ever known, or that it refused to give equality to its thirteen million black citizens. However, the fact remained that America had begun an antiliberal, antidemocratic retreat from its ideals.

The U.S. Supreme Court in the postwar period did

strike down laws denying equality to black people. However, during the administration of President Harry S Truman, terrorist acts against blacks even increased. Masses of blacks suffered age-old indignities and brutalities at the time Paul and Lawrence Brown were on a successful concert tour across America. Paul had reached his peak as a singer but he was in the throes of the most prolonged, unhappy mood Lawrence Brown had ever seen. His voice was better than ever; yet Paul wasn't satisfied. Often, he felt he couldn't walk on one more stage or sing another concert.

He wanted to tell the huge, adoring audiences what was happening to his black people and to minority peoples of the world. For example, the Supreme Court had ruled that interstate buses traveling from state to state must permit blacks to sit anywhere. But Paul knew that if they dared sit anywhere but the rear of a bus, they might be beaten senseless or even murdered. Supreme Court rulings affecting blacks were worthless if they were not enforced. How was he to say this from the concert stage? Maybe he should leave the stage so that he could say whatever he wanted.

But for the time being, he gave up the idea of leaving public life and gave himself over more and more to the public. He went on singing and voicing his opinions whenever he could.

Lawrence Brown admitted to biographer Marie Seton that Paul never had a personal life except when he went to sleep.

Paul had said, "I think I always knew from my youth around my father's church that I belonged to the community and that my life would never be a very personal one."

If there was not much of a private Paul, there was something to be said for the style of the public one. In September 1946, he was one of the sponsors of a national conference against lynching. The conference was a coalition of some fifty organizations. It sent del-

egates to Washington to discuss anti-lynching legislation with President Truman. As one of the delegates,
Paul was about to meet the President for the first
time. And face to face, he read a statement asking Mr.
Truman to pronounce a "formal public statement"
that would make clear his views on lynching. Moreover, Mr. Truman was to establish a "definite legislative and educational program to end the disgrace of
mob violence."[9]

The New York Times buried Paul's interpretation of
the President's reply on page 60:

> The President, according to Mr. Robeson, indi-
> cated that political matters made it difficult to
> issue a statement of his views at this time. As to
> possible Federal legislation to curb lynching, Mr.
> Robeson said the President expressed the view
> that passage was a political matter in which tim-
> ing was important. The President took exception,
> Mr. Robeson asserted, to a suggestion by the del-
> egation that it "seemed inept for the United
> States to take the lead in the Nuremberg trials
> and fall so far behind in respect to justice to Ne-
> groes in this country." . . .
>
> Mr. Robeson also said the President termed
> America and Great Britain the last refuge of free-
> dom in the world. "I disagreed with this," said
> Robeson. "The British Empire is one of the great-
> est enslavers of human beings." He declared that
> American and British policy today were "not sup-
> porting anti-fascism."[10]

Paul was then asked by a reporter if he was a Communist. He said no, adding, "I label myself as very
violently antifascist."

So it was that his very real concern for black and
poor people became confused in the minds of the
public with communism. In less than a month, the
California Legislative Committee on Un-American
Activities would subpoena him in order to discover

just how communist he had become, at which time he would tell it that he was not a member of the Communist Party. Later on, however, he would refuse to answer that question. He would cite the Fifth Amendment to the Constitution, which holds that no American can be compelled to be a witness against himself.

But no matter how honestly he spoke, the relentless forces of slander would tighten like a noose about his neck.

Paul Robeson had always been an honorable and an unselfish man. As the distinguished black leaders who had honored him with the Spingarn Medal had said, he was a man of the highest spirit, he was a noble man. He earned hundreds of thousands of dollars—and forwent just as many thousands which he could have earned by refusing to say what people expected a member of a downtrodden race might well have said: *Yes, sir, America's been good to me. Any black man can make it to the top if he keeps on smiling and acts the way he's supposed to...*

He never acted the way he was supposed to and never masked his feelings in order to advance himself. He did what he had to do to further what he termed a social revolution that would bring about not only racial equality in his own country but equality and independence for colonial peoples in Africa. If he was to become a mournful, calamitous figure draped in melancholy, as so many of the sympathetic were to describe him, the tragedy wasn't his alone. It was more a country's which could no longer accept free speech, although that was its ideal; nor dissent, which is the embodiment of its democracy.

There was an increase in tensions between the Soviet Union and the United States with the announcement of the Truman Doctrine in 1947. Since there was evidence that Greece and Turkey might fall to Communist pressure, President Truman declared on March 12, 1947, a national policy to "contain" Communist expansion by supplying military equipment and profes-

sional military advisers to Greece and Turkey. The
U.S. would hereafter assist peoples anywhere to pre-
vent capture of their governments by what Mr. Truman called "minority parties."

At home in America, it was believed there was danger of infiltration of Communist spies into government departments, such as the Department of State
and the Department of Defense. There had been actual betrayals of technical data relating to the atomic
bomb. To guard against more betrayals, the Truman
Administration subjected all federal employees to a
continuing examination of their loyalty to the U.S.,
with the help of the Federal Bureau of Investigation.
The personal opinions and conduct of American citizens who were government employees were
"screened." Their membership in organizations listed
by the Attorney General as subversive were "looked
into," thus applying the principle of *guilt by association.* One might be innocent of communist ideology
but if one had friends who were linked to so-called
subversive organizations, one was termed a *fellow
traveler* and under suspicion—or in some cases,
guilty—for knowing them.

During this period, America's fear of the USSR and
concern with citizen loyalty to the U.S. grew to alarming proportions. The personal freedom to which
America was supposed to be committed was in grave
danger of being destroyed.

Such checking on personal political opinions spilled
over into areas outside of government. The labor unions
soon expelled members and officers who appeared to
be pro-Soviet. Without justification, about half of the
country imposed loyalty oaths on its public school and
college teachers. So it happened that anyone at home
in America sympathetic to the Soviet union and communism had a difficult time, indeed.

By the spring of 1947, Paul had made it quite clear
as to where he stood in relation to America and the
Soviet Union. He loved his country but he despised its
bigotry and brutality with all the despair and anger of

an outcast native son. He admired the Soviet Union because of his impression of it as a land of equality for all peoples. This ideal was forever a part of his vision. He believed that "socialism" (his term) was a higher form of government, economically and morally superior to a "system based upon production for private profit."[1]

He went to St. Louis for a benefit concert. Later, he joined the Civil Rights Congress picket line in front of the American Theatre there, which practiced racial segregation.

Besides the Russian, Chinese, French and Italian songs he always sang, and the black spirituals, he began to sing what he termed songs of free men. At the University of Utah, Paul sang the stirring "Ballad of Joe Hill":

> *I dreamed I saw Joe Hill last night,*
> *Alive as you and me.*
> *Says I, "But Joe you're ten years dead,"*
> *"I never died," says he.*
> *"I never died," says he. . . .*
>
> *And standing there as big as life*
> *And smiling with his eyes,*
> *Says Joe, "What they forgot to kill*
> *Went on to organize,*
> *Went on to organize."[2]*

Joe Hill had been a union organizer and was executed for murder in the Utah State Penitentiary. His union friends insisted he had never committed the murder, that he had been framed. Thus, he became a hero to the tough miners in the copper mines.

After singing "Joe Hill," Paul told his audience that he wouldn't sing on the concert stage again. But he would, he said, sing for his college and "trade union friends" who always allowed him to sing what he chose to sing.

He had said as much before, but now people

seemed to take him at his word. At least, reaction against him began to gain strength. He was scheduled to appear in Peoria, Illinois, at the Shrine Mosque. On the 3rd of April, the Shriners canceled the contract for the use of the Mosque. The Mayor of Peoria refused to allow the use of City Hall, while the American Legion (a politically conservative group) loudly protested Paul's scheduled appearance. Finally, those opposed to him both as a black man and as a man of ideas succeeded in stopping the public from hearing him.

This was the first time such an attempt had been made but it would not be the last. On May 9, Paul was scheduled to give a concert at Philip Livingston Junior High School in Albany, New York. The Albany Board of Education denied permission for having the concert in the school.

A black Methodist church group, the Carver Cultural Society, was the sponsor of the concert. And the group immediately took legal action against the Board of Education to protect Paul's civil rights. For two weeks, the legal battle took place in the courtroom of Supreme Court Justice Isadore Bookstein between the citizens of Albany and the Board of Education.

On May 6, Justice Bookstein issued a legal order restraining the Albany Board from interfering with Paul's concert:

> Defendant's [Bd. of Education] only asserted reason for its action is the political philosophy or ideology of Robeson. That philosophy or ideology, however objectionable to the vast majority of American citizens, has nothing to do with the purposes for which the permit was originally granted, to wit, a musical concert.[3]

Justice Bookstein had perhaps made a serious mistake in his assumption as to what Paul's "political philosophy" and "ideology" actually were. Even so, he was able to make a correct judgment concerning the case before him. He prohibited the Board from revoking the permit for Paul to use the school auditorium. Paul's concert took place as scheduled. The Albany American Legion called for a boycott of the concert and set up pickets at the building. Eleven hundred people came anyway to hear Paul sing. He sang but made no political remarks; the concert was a great success, with the audience extremely responsive.

Paul completed tour commitments outside of trade union circles amid critical demands that he stop making propaganda from the stage. He spent a short time in New York and at The Beeches in Connecticut. And then he went off on another concert tour, this time to Panama, where he was to give four concerts for the United Public Workers of America. The UPW was trying to unionize Panamanian workers who were predominantly black. The tickets for his concerts were selling for just a dollar apiece. With tickets so cheap, anti-union people hinted that he was being paid by mysterious and unknown forces to come to Panama just to cause trouble.

But in fact, tickets had been priced low because the union sponsors knew they could bring out vast numbers of people. They were right, for an audience of ten thousand turned out for a single Robeson concert.

His concerts were tremendous events at which he sang and played parts from *Othello*. He also voiced his opinions, which by now he was used to doing. In 1946, before the State of California's Tenney Committee on Un-American Activities, he had said that real racial equality was "almost not an American conception. If Mr. Truman is going to raise the underprivileged third of the nation, or the Negro one-tenth, he'd better establish a dictatorship in the South."[4]

The general public in 1947 was still not used to hearing nonwhites speak the way Paul did. He had never been one to plead or beg, so what he said to the California politicians was thought to be militantly revolutionary: "As a Negro in America, I can speak here today, but I could go down to Georgia tomorrow and be dead."[4]

He had been called before the California Tenney Committee because of his affiliation with organizations which demanded immediate racial equality for black Americans. And as a member of the National Committee to Win the Peace, and of the Civil Rights Congress, he didn't care that the Tenney Committee thought these groups Communist-organized and Communist-controlled. Moreover, Paul became acquainted with the International Longshoremen's and Warehousemen's Union because at the time this union was dedicated to racial equality. The ILWU was considered pro-Communist, and he left himself open to more accusations. Under ILWU sponsorship, he went to Hawaii to sing in Honolulu and then to island-hop, giving concerts in smaller towns and cities.

This type of suspicious reaction to Paul proved somewhat embarrassing for the American government, which had used him to promote the war effort during World War II and which liked to portray the country as a melting pot of peace- and freedom-loving citizens. But political conservatives were expressing their fear of people different from themselves, in color as well as ideas. In the summer of 1947, the American Legion of Peekskill, New York, urged a boycott of Paul's summer concert there. Next, a Congressional committee which considered itself the "watchdog" against Communism, the House Un-American Activities Committee (HUAC), issued a report listing him as one of the sponsors of so-called Communist-front organizations. HUAC proposed legislation that would outlaw the Communist Party from the United States, legislation which President Truman thought unconstitutional.

The Truman Administration had subtly used the fear of communism in 1946–47 to further its foreign policy. Its campaign for the Marshall Plan to lend money to the war-shattered economies of Europe (the Euro-

an Recovery Program) increased the clamor of anti-
mmunist emotions to an alarming degree:

> Until the free nations of Europe have regained
> their strength, and so long as Communism threat-
> ens the very existence of democracy, the United
> States must remain strong enough to support
> those countries of Europe which are threatened
> with Communist control and police-state rule.[5]

By 1948, distrust of Communism abroad had wid-
ned into distrust of all manner of dissent at home.
Truman now watched helplessly as his political op-
onents took charge of the anticommunist issue and
itiated the period of McCarthyism."[*6]
What was foremost in Paul Robeson's thinking was
at he must help make blacks full citizens in Amer-
a. To accomplish this, he would need to become al-
ost totally a political person. For the overriding senti-
ent in America during this period was the fear of
d battle over communism, which overshadowed the
sue of civil rights for blacks.
He was certain that his singing would never open
e hearts of white Americans to his cause of black
eedom. And he suspected that art changed nothing.
or as an artist and a performer, he was not supposed
speak his mind from the concert stage. All such lec-
uring was thought best left to the politicians. So it
as that when a new and large, well-financed third
olitical party became a strong possibility, he at once
ecame a part of it.
Late in January 1948, he attended a meeting in New
ork where others, also, had gathered to form the na-
onal Wallace for President Committee. The Commit-

The term McCarthyism is derived from the political rhetoric
: Senator Joseph McCarthy of Wisconsin during the early
950's. It was a way of making dissent seem like disloyalty to the
.S. and loyalty to the USSR. The association of dissent with
ommunism and the public accusation of pro-communism was
ost often unsupported by proof.

tee hoped to persuade Henry A. Wallace to run fo
President of the United States in the November elec
tion campaign.

Henry A. Wallace had been Secretary of Agricultur
under President Roosevelt and was Vice-President i
Roosevelt's third term. He was dismissed from his po
sition as Secretary of Commerce in the Truman Ac
ministration in 1946, because he opposed Truman
"get tough with Russia" policy. One of the editors c
The New Republic, a liberal weekly magazine, he wa
perhaps the man who was well known enough and c
the right political persuasion to build a third politica
party.

Out of the January 1948 meeting developed the Pro
gressive Party. And in the 1948 election the Progre
sive Party would offer a platform of domestic reform
Its foreign policy program was opposed to the Ma
shall Plan for Europe. Furthermore, its members hel
the belief that the United States could get along wit
the Soviet Union.

Just a few months later, Paul traveled over th
country speaking for Henry Wallace and informing th
public that the Progressive Party stood for equa
rights. He introduced Mr. Wallace at a party organiza
tional meeting in Chicago; he was asked to run fo
Vice-President but felt it necessary to decline. An
from April until July, he was on a political tour o
behalf of Henry Wallace. However, he and the Pro
gressive Party were not the only ones out barnstorm
ing.

There were at least a dozen separate political par
ties introduced on the 1948 ballot and out campaign
ing for national office. There were states' righter
southern conservatives; there were liberals, progres
sives, communists. People who feared the Progressiv
Party's ideals of social and racial equality often at
tempted to confuse it for the public with the Com
munist Party. And those who held political ideals sim
ilar to Henry Wallace's were harassed as wer

members of the Communist Party. Such a situation eventually hurt the Progressives severely.

A parade of dissimilar political groups was out on the campaign trail. The public couldn't tell to whom to listen. Public opinion and speechmaking, also, were loud but not at all clear.

Paul spoke before many union groups who had invited him to their conventions. Yet, he was stopped from speaking at the convention of the Transport Workers Union in New York because union leader Michael Quill, like so many others, thought Paul was being controlled by Communists. Authorities in West Virginia succeeded in banning *Paul Robeson: Citizen of the World,* a children's biography of Paul by Shirley Graham. Because of Paul's left-wing political views, the biography was kept out of the public libraries.

Thus, in the spring and summer of 1948, democracy in America underwent a severe test. Sympathy toward the Soviet Union and toward communism was becoming increasingly unpopular. Anti-communist legislation was being prepared. The Mundt–Nixon bill (cosponsored by Richard Nixon, who became President of the U.S. in 1968) attempted to halt the spread of communism by requiring many organizations suspected of being Communist to register with the Justice Department.

President Truman began to indicate that anticommunist emotion had reached alarming levels. To a Chicago audience, he said that the "menace of communism lies primarily in the areas of American life where the promise of democracy remains unfulfilled."[7]

Yet investigations of "subversives" flourished in this period. The House Un-American Activities Committee kept up its watch on communism, as did the similar Senate committee. Many citizens were brought to Washington to testify before various anticommunist committees as to their own loyalty to America and to the loyalty of their friends. José Ferrer, nominated for an Academy Award for his role in *Cyrano de Bergerac*, was one such citizen. Former Iago to Paul Robeson's Othello, Ferrer "came on like a penitent fox that had just renounced its appetite for fowl."[8] He said his name had been misused by Communist-front groups. He hadn't seen that great friend of Russia, Paul Robeson, for six years.

Numerous citizens, when they refused to state their political views—when asked whether they were or had ever been Communists—were cited for contempt of Congress and sent to jail. For the first time in this century, America allowed its citizens to be jailed in time of peace for their *political* beliefs. The Executive Secretary of the Communist Party, Eugene Dennis, was cited for contempt. Ten filmwriters faced jail for refusing to answer questions concerning their politics.

It must be kept in mind that many people, not only those accused, believed as Paul Robeson did, that the government was infringing on the Constitutional rights of American citizens. They were defended variously under the First, Fifth and Fourteenth Amendments of the Constitution. As yet, it was *not* illegal to belong to *any* political party.

Paul Robeson thought America would throw away all those truths she had once held to be self-evident: the equality of all and the right of all to life and liberty. Never one to sit back while others acted upon what he believed to be right, he went to Washington to testify before the Senate hearings on the Mundt–Nixon Communist-control bill. He knew that if he failed to answer the questions satisfactorily, he could be cited for contempt of Congress. Nonetheless, he felt he had to go to fight for the democracy and freedom that were his dream.

The Mundt–Nixon bill drafted by the House Un-American Activities Committee provided:

1. That all Communist Party members register, be declared ineligible for Federal Employment, be denied passports, and be subject to immediate deportation if aliens.
2. That all "Communist Front" organizations (as defined by the Attorney General) be compelled to register and keep contributors' and membership files available for official requisition.
3. That the Attorney General be the sole finder of facts as to "Communist Front" organizations, and that his findings of fact be not subject to review by the courts.[1]

On May 14, 1948, Congressman Vito Marcantonio of East Harlem, New York, spoke out against the bill. He said if it passed, it would:

> change the form of government under which we have lived for over 150 years. . . . What is really the issue here is the Constitution. What is really involved here is whether or not we intend to preserve our Bill of Rights. The question before the House is whether or not we shall have the courage to defend the democratic traditions of our Nation, and the democratic foundations on which our Government is based, despite the hysteria

which is mounting every day to the accompaniment of the fast beating of war drums.[2]

Mr. Marcantonio's plea went unheeded. On May 19, 1948, the House passed the Mundt–Nixon bill by a vote of 319 to 58 with 34 abstentions. The Senate had to vote next.

Paul Robeson went to Washington on June 1 to appear before the Senate Committee holding hearings on the Mundt–Nixon bill. Late in the day, the hearings were "indefinitely recessed" because opponents of the bill had been shouting that they would bring "thousands" to the capital city to demonstrate heartily against it. However, before the hearings were recessed, Paul got his chance to testify.

On taking the stand, he was asked more than once by the Committee's Chairman, Senator Ferguson, whether he was a Communist. Each time, he said he would "answer that" when he came to it. Finally, the Senator asked Paul again, "Are you a Communist?"

Paul answered: "The question has become the very basis of the struggle for civil liberties. Nineteen men are about to go to jail for refusing to answer it. I am prepared to join them. I refuse to answer it."[3]

At that moment, Paul could have been cited for contempt; but he was not, Senator Ferguson later told a reporter, because a committee quorum had not been present when the question was asked.

Paul was next questioned as to whether he thought American communists would be loyal to the United States if America ever went to war with the Soviet Union.

He said, "I would think that the struggle would be for peace."

Then, he was asked if he would fight for the United States in a war with the Soviet Union.

"That would depend on conditions," Paul said.

Senator Ferguson asked him, "If Congress declared war on Russia, would you fight for the United States?"

Paul answered: "I would say that's too hypothetical. That would depend on many things."

"Then you would be the judge?" asked another senator of the Committee.

"No, no," Paul said. "A lot of people would be the judges."[3]

The Senate Committee lacked a quorum and so Paul was not held in contempt nor thrown into jail. The Senators on the Committee might have been relieved by the fact, since 1948 was an election year. Both Republicans and Democrats wanted the Negro vote, and putting the great Robeson in jail would have unleashed a wave of black and white liberal protest, which could have benefited only the new Progressive Party.

The next day, Paul joined with thousands who had swarmed into the capital to defeat the Mundt–Nixon bill. There were also civil rights advocates who had come in hopes of seeing a civil rights program enacted before Congress recessed.

Pickets five and six deep were lined across the entrance to the White House, and others were stationed outside the headquarters of the Democratic and Republican National Committees. Hundreds more sought out their states' congressmen hoping for direct confrontation in order to influence the senators in favor of their cause.

That night, at a rally on the slopes surrounding the Washington Monument, Paul was presented to the thousands gathered. He sang, in the words of *The New York Times*, "three militantly political songs" and then "cried out to the crowd":

> The struggle for peace and the kind of America we want has reached another level; we have taken the offensive against fascism! We will take the power from their hands and through our representatives we will direct the future destiny of our nation.[4]

* * *

At least one biographer has said that at this time,
Paul's singing was far more political than musical. His
concert managers were indeed receiving ever-
increasing numbers of complaints from small-town
tour managers. However, audiences still turned out
enthusiastically to hear him. But charges that he presented "more politics than music" were always made
by critics when he appeared before groups considered
left-wing or communist. Such was the case when on
June 23 he appeared at a Manhattan Center dinner
sponsored by the literary publication *Masses and
Mainstream.* Also appearing that night were the writers John Howard Lawson and Howard Fast, both
cited for contempt by the House Un-American Activities Committee for not answering questions as to their
politics and their friends. HUAC thought it had information that John Howard Lawson was one of the
most active Communist screenwriters in Hollywood.
According to Lawson's own statement, after appearing
before the Committee:

> I am not going to touch on the gross violation of
> the Constitution of the United States, and espe-
> cially of its First and Fifth Amendments, that is
> taking place here. The proof is so overwhelming
> that it needs no elaboration. The Un-American
> Activities Committee stands convicted in the
> court of public opinion. . . .
>
> My political and social views are well known.
> My deep faith in the motion picture as a popular
> art is also well known. I don't "sneak ideas" into
> pictures. . . . I will never permit what I write
> and think to be subject to the orders of self-
> appointed dictators, ambitious politicians,
> thought-control gestapos, or any other form of
> censorship this Un-American Committee may at-
> tempt to devise.[5]

The fact that Paul was willing to stand up in public
with Lawson made him an even more controversial

figure. On the night of June 23, he said that all artists and writers must oppose the Mundt–Nixon bill and any such legislation that would destroy civil liberties in America. Howard Fast said, according to *The New York Times,* that the "proponents of the bill should be thrown out of the national scene as 'obscene human beings.'"

Denunciation of Mundt–Nixon continued and the pressure from opponents of it became so great that the Senate did not bring it to a vote. Thus, the bill did not become law and the forces for civil liberty had won their battle against it.

Yet, there would be other bills and other battles, and there was no time to savor this one victory. Thousands who fought against Mundt–Nixon now had to turn their attention to national politics and the presidential election campaign of 1948. The two major parties held their conventions in Philadelphia. The Republicans nominated the Governor of New York, Thomas E. Dewey, for President, and for Vice-President the Governor of California, Earl Warren. The Democrats nominated President Harry S Truman for re-election, and Senator Alben W. Barkley of Kentucky for Vice-President.

At the end of July, the new Progressive Party held its convention and nominated Henry Wallace for President of the United States and Senator Glen H. Taylor for Vice-President. The keynote address for this national convention was given by a black man, a lawyer, Charles Howard.

The Progressive Party soon gained momentum and followers across the country. In New York, Representative Vito Marcantonio hailed Henry Wallace as the political descendent of Franklin Delano Roosevelt. Furthermore, Marcantonio declared that the American Labor Party, of which he was an elected official in the House of Representatives, would endorse Mr. Wallace for President.

Almost at once, "red-baiting" of the Progressive Party began. Many people believed that Communists had control of the Progressive Party, that it endorsed the foreign policy of the Soviet Union and that its platform included almost all of the recommendations of the U.S. Communist Party.

> The Americans for Democratic Action, fearing that Wallace might split the liberal vote and thus hand the victory to [Republican-Party candidate] Dewey, tried to use guilt-by-association tactics by printing in major urban newspapers the names of the Progressive party's principal contributors and then listing the organizations on the Attorney General's list of subversive groups to which these contributors belonged—or had belonged.[6]

At the Democratic convention, liberals and big-city bosses proposed a stronger statement on civil rights than the one President Truman supported. The stronger statement won approval by the convention, although some southern delegations did walk out in protest. President Truman, noting later the vast drawing power of Henry Wallace and Paul Robeson at political gatherings all over America, realized that unhappy Republicans and Democrats were extremely interested in having a new and vital domestic political policy. With this in mind, Mr. Truman in his own campaign adopted some of the social and racial stands of the Progressive Party and shifted to the left on domestic policy.

In every state, election laws were being used by both major parties to keep the Progressive Party off the ballot. Moreover, President Truman began telling black voters that he would, if elected, introduce a Civil Rights Bill. He had already sent a civil rights message to Congress on February 2, 1948, which was partly "inspired by fear of Henry Wallace, who had recently announced his candidacy for President on the Progressive party ticket and who seemed likely to lure five million liberal voters from the Democrats."[7] The Republicans said that the Democrats might as well hand over the country to the Communists, since they had so quickly sold out.

Thus, the 1948 campaign with its implied bigotry, its cynicism, became absolutely wild with accusations.

Meanwhile, Paul Robeson and Henry Wallace were on a dangerous and widely publicized campaign sweep through the South. Paul was forced to speak to segregated audiences, in union halls and black churches. He was threatened with lynching and Wallace was pelted with tomatoes and rotten eggs. On one such trip, the treasurer of the Progressive Party, who was white, had to describe himself as a "white Negro" in order to sit with Paul and Lawrence Brown in a railroad car designated for Negroes only.

As was his wont, Paul spoke out for black equality and against oppression everywhere. He made an overwhelmingly favorable impression by what he said and the songs he sang—great, moving melodies such as "Ol' Man River" and "Go Down, Moses." But the Progressive Party never had the opportunity to capture a large portion of the American vote. When it came time to vote, the disenchanted, fairly conservative former Republicans and Democrats were too frightened to vote for a party whose leaders were called Communists and communist sympathizers by major American magazines and newspapers. The Progressive Party, however, had forced Truman and the Democrats to become more liberal and to give more than lip service to the civil liberties of blacks.

On election day, more blacks voted for Truman than voted for Henry Wallace. Even though black people were terribly proud of Paul, they refused to follow him all the way along his political path. When he spoke out for their cause, they found him overpowering. But when he spoke warmly of the Soviet Union, of socialism, they, like so many other Americans, distrusted what he said.

In the final voting, Henry Wallace ran ahead of Socialist Party candidate Norman Thomas, but behind the white supremacist candidate of the States' Rights

Party, Strom Thurmond. Truman was re-elected to the presidency, with a popular vote of twenty-four million to Governor Dewey's twenty-two million votes.

Wallace's election showing was disappointing to Progressive Party leaders, for he had run poorly among the black population as well as the white liberal one. Soon, organizations and individuals began to desert the Progressive Party, including Henry Wallace himself. By early fall, 1950, he had completely severed ties with the Progressive Party movement.

Nevertheless, Paul held to his beliefs as he always had. But having been a leader in the progressive thrust for civil liberties and equality, he became a target for retreating liberals and radicals who found themselves wounded on the political battlefield. In the winter of 1948, the Transport Workers Union withdrew its invitation to have Paul attend its convention. For ten years, Paul had regularly attended the convention and held an honorary life membership in the Union. This single, petty act was definitely a forecast of things to come.

"I came here to sing and for you to sing with me," is the closing line of an epic poem, "Let The Rail-Splitter Awake," by Paul's friend the Chilean poet Pablo Neruda. The poem, Paul once wrote, spoke for him, also. He had not sung formally in concert since that time in Albany when he was denied permission and then allowed to sing because of a court ruling in his favor. He'd wanted to sing as he wished, he had said then. Throughout all of the political battles of 1947 and 1948, he had spoken and sung for progress and for his people. His involvement in organized politics was for the time at an end, and he wished again to appear on the concert stage. Yet he refused to simply sing and leave his political views at home. According to the *San Francisco Chronicle*, eighty concerts arranged for the 1949–50 season were unceremoniously canceled by nervous concert managers.

Paul left the country in February 1949, to give two concerts in London. The concerts were overwhelmingly successful. He went on to Manchester, and tickets for 10,000 seats put on sale in the morning were all sold by noon. He saw "people obviously not the regular concert goers, and even workers in seats they must have sacrificed a lot to get."[8]

This was Paul's first visit to England in ten years, and he breathed freely again.

Time, which works against the artist, especially the singer, had been good to Paul. He had left England a decade earlier a star and he returned now, still a star. But his eyes had been opened by events. He was as much aware of his own political development as he was of his artistic maturity. He sang all over England through February and March, to small groups and to the vast audiences of ten thousand and more.

However, by the end of April, he was embroiled in a controversy that caused him considerable personal damage.

It happened in Paris on Wednesday, April 20. The many-tiered Salle Pleyel was to be the meeting place for the Paris World Congress of Partisans of Peace. Delegates from sixty countries had come to express their hopes for peace, representing peoples from all over the world. The great black scholar and writer Dr. W.E.B. Du Bois was there and later made arrangements to have dinner with Paul in the Pleyel's gilt-and-mirror-paneléd dinner salon.

When Paul entered the Salle Pleyel, the program was interrupted as hundreds of delegates to the Congress rose to cheer him in a multitude of languages. Paul went to the podium as had other delegates throughout the conference. A moment's silence, and then he sang, his great, deep voice rising in songs of black slaves, songs of Russia and of France. Then he spoke informally to this noonday gathering of delegates.

A London group representing some six hundred million colored peoples had asked Paul to represent them in Paris at the Peace Congress and to say that they did not want war. The group was known as the

Coordinating Committee of Colonial Peoples and was sponsored by the President of the South African Indian Congress, Dr. Y.M. Dadoo.

Paul had addressed the Coordinating Committee on the occasion of its conference against South African apartheid (segregation). No sooner had he done so than the South African radio network banned his records from the air. He had also angered some Americans at home but for different reasons.

(Paul had mentioned to reporters that he would return to the U.S. to testify as a witness for eleven members of the Executive Committee of the U.S. Communist Party on trial for violating the Smith Act. The Act was a law passed in 1940 as part of the anticommunist feeling in America. It made it unlawful for any person to advocate, or teach to advocate, the overthrow of the United States government by force or violence, or to organize or become a member of any group dedicated to teaching such doctrine. It was directed against the Communist Party. The eleven Party defendants were alleged to have reorganized the Communist Party in 1945 for this purpose and on orders from Moscow. But Paul believed that Marxism was a cultural philosophy and that a philosophy was on trial unjustly. His stand in support of the Communist defendants mystified and angered many people.)

It could be said that in Paris, when Paul stood to speak to the delegates of the World Congress of Peace, his critics were poised to react. The hundreds who filled the Salle Pleyel from floor to rafters listened intently as Paul said:

> It is unthinkable that American Negroes would go to war on behalf of those who have oppressed us for generations [against the Soviet Union] which in one generation has raised our people to full human dignity.[9]

No other statement he ever made created such furor. His words went immediately to America and were almost at once distorted. He was quoted in *The New York Times* on April 24: "Mr. Robeson told the [Peace] congress that American Negroes never would fight against the Soviet Union." Out of context, this was a distortion of his words.

A former Robeson friend and associate in the Council on African Affairs and the National Negro Congress, Max Yergan, was first to denounce Paul's Paris statement:

> The counterpart of Mr. Paul Robeson's Russian idol, the American Communist Party, certainly has not "raised our people to the full dignity of mankind." [Yergan quotes here from *Crisis* quote of Robeson's statement, which reads, "which in one generation has raised our people to the full dignity of mankind."]
>
> I know some Negro Communists. Few of them are individuals who have experienced the "full dignity of mankind." . . .
>
> It is the grossest travesty upon truth to say that these miserable cowards and hirelings have been raised "to the full dignity of mankind." These are the only Negroes that American Communists have influenced. Fortunately, their duplicity has never touched the majority of the Negro population.[10]

Walter White, Executive Secretary of the National Association for the Advancement of Colored People (NAACP) said: "Negroes contend for full and equal rights and we accept full and equal responsibilities. In any conflict involving our nation we will regard ourselves as Americans and meet the responsibilities imposed on all Americans."[11] Other blacks and whites, also, considered Robeson a traitor for his remarks in Paris, believing that he represented no one, least of all some fifteen million black Americans.

However, the main point of Paul's Paris statement—

the struggle for peace—was rarely quoted. He had said:

> We colonial peoples have contrbuted to the build-
> ing of the United States and are determined to
> share in its wealth. We denounce the policy of the
> U.S. Government which is similar to that of Hit-
> ler and Goebbels. We want peace and liberty and
> will combat for them along with the Soviet Union,
> the democracies of Eastern Europe, China and
> Indonesia.[12]

Obviously, the issue of genocide and the compari-
son of the United States with that of Hitler's Third
Reich could have made for a serious argument and
criticism of Paul's point of view. But what seemed to
upset Americans a great deal more than his calling his
country fascist was that he had separated blacks into
some mysterious *black movement distinct from the
rest of America.*

Always, blacks had been thought to be loyal to
America, but here was an enormously respected and
famous black man saying that they might not feel
loyal in the least to a country that had traditionally
oppressed them.

For a decade, Paul had taken on the mantle of
spokesman for American blacks. And for the most
part, blacks had not minded. No matter what he said
or did in their behalf, they remained justly proud of
his great talent and accomplishments. But now, they
felt compelled to speak out as to whether they agreed
with him. Many prominent black leaders continued to
deny that Paul spoke for their people. But a year later
Dr. W.E.B. Du Bois, who had heard Paul's Paris statement, wrote in *Negro Digest:*

> I agree with Paul Robeson absolutely, that Ne-
> groes should never willingly fight in an unjust
> war. I do not share his honest hope that all will
> not. A certain sheeplike disposition, inevitably

born of slavery, will, I am afraid, lead many of them to join America in any enterprise, provided the whites will grant them equal right to do wrong.[13]

In another section of the same article, Walter White denied that Paul spoke for black Americans:

What makes Paul Robeson's wrongness more inexplicable is the surrender of his excellent and honest Phi Beta Kappa mind to the vagaries, reversals, contradictions and plain downright dishonesties of the Communist Party line.[14]

Yet Mr. White ended his statement with these words:

And one of the fundamental tenets of that free society for which we strive is to continue to assure to the Paul Robesons what Voltaire is reputed to have promised, "I disagree with everything you say but I will fight to the death for your right to say it."[15]

But in April of 1949, not all Americans were willing to extend to Paul the right of free speech. On the 23rd, in Hartford, Connecticut, the Chairman of the State Development Commission made a formal request to the State Police Commissioner to keep Paul out of Connecticut if he should try to visit his home, The Beeches, in Enfield. The request was denied.

The Chairman of the Commission was quoted in *The New York Times* on April 24 as having been "disgusted with the remarks Mr. Robeson made at the Communist-dominated world peace congress in Paris."

By this time, Paul was in Sweden, where he gave a concert. Although the concert was a success, for the first time he was booed when he sang songs praising communism and revolution.

Paul went on to Oslo, Norway, for still another con-

cert where he declared he would devote himself from
now on to making political speeches and that this
would probably be his last concert trip to Europe.

And hurt by the clamor against him, particularly
from many of his own people in America, he said
somewhat sadly that he foresaw the day when his
opinions and speeches would land him in jail.

The year 1949 marked the end of America's en-
thrallment with Paul Robeson. For some of his countrymen evidently thought they could no longer safely
enjoy the magnificence of his great voice. The man
had become dangerously "subversive" and the man,
along with the voice, had to be stilled.

Paul Robeson has been variously described as politically naive and as a political adolescent for not being more critical of Soviet Communism. But as writer and critic Eric Bentley has written:

> It was Robeson the political activist that provided the American Establishment with the opportunity to see if it, like the Soviet authorities, could make an unperson of someone. . . . Robeson kept being rebuked for mixing up civil rights with Marxism. But in *that* "mix-up" he today seems farsighted and not at all wrong-headed.[1]

Paul's point of view was not unlike that of third world peoples, particularly Asians, who did not accept Soviet Communism completely, or American capitalism either. Rather, they wished to bring together the best qualities of both.

He was far more concerned with the Soviet Union's professed principle of racial equality than with its political ideology. As Eric Bentley wrote, where Paul may have gotten "mixed up" was "in identifying Marx and Stalin. But this confusion was hardly a personal eccentricity of Paul Robeson's—rather, the historic error of the world Communist movement in his time."[2]

Paul believed he could change the course of the history of downtrodden peoples by appealing to the moral principles of humanity. At the very least, he felt he must fight racism around the world with the tools available to a single individual well known enough to make himself heard.

For him, a black man, the ultimate goal of a true democracy had to be equality. And the fight for it was immensely more real to him than his country's fear of Soviet Communism. Paul would never back down in a fight, when what he said or what he sang turned powerful governments against him. He stirred the hearts of vast numbers of people. And while they did not always agree with him, they were awed by his prophetic voice and his personal nobility.

On tour in Europe in 1949, he worked his way toward the Soviet Union and Moscow, in hopes of seeing again the Russian people whom he loved dearly. His vision of the Soviets had remained that of a nation which had conscientiously rid itself of racial prejudice.

At the end of May, he gave concerts in Prague and in Warsaw. In Poland, he visited what was left of the Warsaw Ghetto, where during World War II hundreds upon hundreds of Jews had been systematically starved by their Nazi captors before they were destroyed. As a symbol of Jewish brotherhood, they had fought to the death rather than be divided, conquered and annihilated in Nazi concentration camps.

Paul stood amid the Ghetto rubble. Under his feet lay bits and pieces of Jewish life, all that was left. The desolation of the Warsaw Ghetto profoundly moved him. The killing of men, women and children because of their faith was an unspeakable, diabolical act of terror. Could it happen again, and to the colored races next time? He never forgot what he saw nor the fact that human life has counted for so little.

He left Warsaw for Moscow and he had not visited the Soviet Union for twelve years. The war had intervened and the years of his absence might well have been a generation. Everything had changed in the war-torn city, he found, except the people. Muscovites were still the same, open and friendly. He gave three concerts and took part in the celebration given on the

150th anniversary of the birth of Alexander Sergee-
vitch Pushkin (1799–1837), the renowed poet and
short-story writer whose ancestry was said to include
blacks. He sang "Ol' Man River," changing the words
to mean in Russian, "We must fight to the death for
peace and freedom."

Paul received more acclaim than had been given to
any other American visitor; nearly all of Moscow's
newspapers interviewed him. The journal of the Communist youth, *Komsomoiskaya Pravda*, published a series of articles by Paul entitled "Two Worlds." The
first article told about his trip to the Soviet Union in
1934; in it he wrote: "Your country, dear readers, is
my second Motherland."[3]

But the happy visit had to come to an end. His tour
over, Paul came home to America on the 16th of June.
Now described by *The New York Times* as the "baritone and Communist sympathizer," he arrived at La
Guardia Airport "denouncing the trial of leaders of
the Communist Party as 'a type of domestic fascism.' "[4]

Time magazine also took note of Paul's arrival, de-
picting him as "the burly baritone" who "orated": " 'In
Eastern democracies, the people are happy and singing and are trying to build for peace—while I have to
be met by a police squad.' "[5]

Time ran a New York *Daily News* photograph of
Paul flanked by six uniformed policemen as he
walked from the plane. This "honor guard" was said
to be standard procedure for famous people who were
likely to draw the curious. Whatever the reason for
"New York's Finest," Paul didn't appreciate it. Furthermore, he informed the press which waited for him
that it had distorted everything he had said on his
tour in Europe.

"I prefer to give what I have to say to papers like
the *Daily Worker*," he said.

The following Sunday, Pauli Robeson, who was
now twenty-one, was planning to be married to Marilyn Greenberg, a former classmate from Cornell Uni-

versity. Miss Greenberg was white. Because this would be a marriage between black and white, the press had a field day. Reporters tried to force their way into the wedding, which was to be a small family affair in Harlem. Paul was outraged at this insult to his son's and his family's privacy, and denounced the newsmen once again:

> I have the greatest contempt for the democratic press, and there is something within me which keeps me from breaking your cameras over your heads. . . . This marriage would not have caused any excitement in the Soviet Union.[6]

Newsmen didn't take kindly to Paul's scathing remarks; yet they continued to dog his footsteps. When he appeared the same evening at a rally sponsored by the Council on African Affairs, the press was there:

> That evening, Traveler Robeson . . . [intoned *Time* magazine] sang five songs and spoke for ninety minutes. Sample: ". . . I am born and bred in this America of ours. I want to love it. I love a part of it. But it's up to the rest of America when I shall love it with the same intensity that I love . . . suffering people the world over, in the way that I deeply and intensely love the Soviet people. That burden of proof rests upon America."[7]

Paul went on to say that the eleven Communist leaders on trial for violating the Smith Act were "brave fighters for my freedom" and that their "struggle is our struggle." If these defendants were not freed, he said, then "all Americans can say good-bye to any attempt to secure civil liberties."

The summer of 1949 marked a distinct change in the attitude of the white press toward Paul. Now news articles about him generally called him a "communist sympathizer." The phrase was an extremely vague expression for calling someone a communist without proof. It suggested that Paul couldn't be trusted, that he was tainted by his contact with the Soviet Union and communism. Furthermore, his income had declined dramatically from the $104,000 he had made in 1947. If it had not been for the $30,000 he made for the concert tour in England in 1949, he would have "starved to death" in the next few years.[8] For the noose of slander and reaction now tightened to cut off the breath of his artistic life.

At this time, relations between the Soviet Union and America were more tense than ever, with the danger of civil war in Korea the cause of the extreme stress. After World War II, Korea had been divided into two countries at the thirty-eighth parallel. The north sector, or North Korea, had a communist regime supported by the Soviet Union, while the south sector, South Korea, was a republic supported by the United States. With two vastly different regimes so close together, war between them became a strong possibility.

At home, there was continuing concern about Communist infiltration of government. Alger Hiss was on trial, having been accused of transmitting State Department documents to agents of the Soviet Union in 1937–38. The eleven Communists were on trial, also. When the Soviet Union exploded an atomic bomb, ending America's monopoly of the weapon, the Cold War turned to ice. By the end of July, Robeson said that the Communist Party was the only political party that stood for peace and opposed war. Moreover, he felt that "the rapidly growing power of the Soviet Union in world affairs would become an important factor in aiding the colonial liberation movement. . . ."[9]

American blacks, he said, would not take part in "an imperialist war." But they would be part of the struggle for peace everywhere. As to his own loyalty, Paul said, "The final test is that I am here in America today, fighting for my people whatever the consequences may be, and here I intend to stay."[10]

There can be no question that he had legitimate causes for concern about the direction America was taking. He was a loyal citizen who had the right to his personal political beliefs as well as the right to express them. Yet his fellow Americans seemed to get the jitters every time he opened his mouth, and were intent on stifling him. Perhaps what he never told them quite clearly enough was that he had long begun to identify the problems of blacks in America with the problems facing workers everywhere. And he felt that only Socialism—in the form* it took in the Soviet Union —seriously addressed itself to their grievances.

He also knew that black Americans in the South were denied the vote by the thousands. That his people were segregated, insulted, brutalized every day of their lives—as Dr. Du Bois had said back in 1914, "from the day of our birth to the day of our death." Nothing could change these truths for Paul, and his homeland seemed least of all willing to change them. America's concern seemed to be only with the threat of Communist takeovers, real or imagined, around the world, and attempts at containing them. Communists were everywhere, in government, in classrooms, in motion pictures, America thought in the summer of 1949. And all it had, all it loved, was in imminent danger of being stolen by the Communists.

If what Paul had to say coincided with the American Communist line and what its newspaper, the *Daily Worker*, had to say, then that would have to be a fact of his existence. He knew very well that the similarity of ideas could not make him a Communist any more than it could make another man Paul Robeson.

---

* Soviet Communists believe their definition of the term and their practical system to be true socialism and view all other versions of socialism as reactionary, if not false. Thus, to them, the term "socialism" and "communism" are nearly interchangeable. In the Soviet Union, communism is further described as a *future* state of their society, of which the present Soviet system is an intermediate stage.

In August, Paul was scheduled to give a series of concerts in Upstate New York. What would happen at two of these concerts would cause many to believe that Nazism had suddenly sprouted on American soil. The seeds of bigotry and racial intolerance were not to be sown only in the deep South, where one might have expected them to find fertile soil; but rather, in the city of Peekskill outside of metropolitan New York City.

Paul had given open-air concerts successfully at Peekskill in previous years. Yet in 1948, the typically conservative American Legion post there asked people to stay away from the concert. Most people did stay away. And exactly a year later, on Saturday, August 27, 1949, the fourth Robeson outdoor concert in a series was to take place. Sponsored by the Civil Rights Congress, which was on the Attorney General's list of "subversive" groups, the proceeds were to go to the Harlem Chapter of the Congress. The concert was to be held at Lakeland Acres Picnic Ground in the town of Cortlandt, just outside the city limits of Peekskill.

When it was announced ten days before the event that Paul Robeson would be coming, there was an immediate outcry of protest. One of the protesters was Vincent Boyle, Commander of the William J. Boyle Post of the American Legion (the post was named after his brother, killed in World War II).

Vincent Boyle was an earnest young man, just twenty-four years old, and an electrician. When his brother died in the war, his father had a fatal heart attack on hearing the news. Both father and son were buried in the Catholic cemetery across the highway from Lakeland Acres.

It was Vincent Boyle who write a letter to the Peekskill *Evening Star* on August 23. Later, the letter was cited by the American Civil Liberties Union* as "a

---

* A nonpartisan nationwide agency to defend groups and persons threatened or injured in violation of civil rights. It defended mutually opposed minorities, such as Jews and the Ku Klux Klan, when either group was under attack by undemocratic methods.

calculated act" leading to "a deliberate and premeditated invasion of Cortlandt, mainly by Peekskill men, for the purpose of committing a crime."[11]

The Boyle letter stated:

> The present days seem to be crucial ones for residents of this area with the present epidemic of polio. Now we are being plagued with another, namely, the appearance of Paul Robeson and his Communistic followers, due to appear here August 27th. It is an epidemic because they are coming here to induce others to join their ranks and it is unfortunate that some of the weaker minded are susceptible to their fallacious teachings unless something is done by the loyal Americans of this area.[11]

Boyle said that he was not "intimating violence" but that all should cooperate with the American Legion— "Let us leave no doubt in their minds that they are unwelcome around here either now or in the future."[11]

The *Evening Star* editorial in the same issue stated that the Robeson concert would "consist of an unsavory mixture of song and political talk by one who has described Russia as his 'second motherland' and who has avowed 'the greatest contempt' for the democratic press."[11]

Residents of the Peekskill community had grown weary of the Robeson concerts simply because the concerts brought in thousands of people from New York City and surrounding areas. Moreover, every summer the region was swamped with summer people, such as the workers from the garment industry in New York who rented, bought and built houses and camps and who felt free to associate with black people if they so chose. Mainly Jewish people came, and some blacks. Almost all were liberal-progressive types who were viewed suspiciously as radical or "communist" by some of the year-round residents.

Paul's concert was scheduled for 8:15 P.M. The public started arriving hours earlier, including scores of cars loaded with anti-Robeson American Legionnaires and Legion sympathizers. One of their trucks blocked the Lakeland Acres entrance and then was fortified with a barricade of stones.

Twenty-five men, the advance group of the concert-goers, ran outside the grounds to find themselves face to face with five hundred Legionnaires. The twenty-five were joined by others, making up a force of forty defenders in all. They locked arms; for more than an hour, they held off the Legionnaires bent on destruction. *Time* magazine reported that the defenders "defiantly burst into the chorus of the old radical marching song, 'We Shall Not Be Moved.' Suddenly, chunks of a wooden fence railing sailed into the ranks of the defenders. Hurling stones and brandishing clubs, the [Legionnaires] charged."[12]

The attacking Legionnaires broke through and rushed the concert area, where they destroyed the stage, set the camp chairs on fire and burned sheet music and anything else they could find that would burn. Women and children ran screaming into the woods as the Legionnaires overturned cars and smashed out the windows. As more and more people arrived for the concert, they ran head-on into Legionnaires. Isolated slugging fights turned into a riot involving thousands.

Paul Robeson had been warned away and never arrived for the concert. By the time police came, around ten in the evening, traffic was tied up for miles; men had been taken to the hospital, one with a brain concussion, another with a knife wound.

With the arrival of the police, the mob of Legionnaires melted away in the darkness. Police and FBI agents made no arrests. The next day, local newspapers tried to play down the incident but a storm of protest from Westchester County residents had already begun. *Time* reported:

* * *

The Communist-line Civil Rights Congress, sponsors of the concert, quickly denounced the sorry affair as an attempt to "lynch Robeson." It was hardly that. But it was an example of misguided patriotism and senseless hooliganism, more useful to Communist propaganda than a dozen uninterrupted song recitals by Paul Robeson.[13]

A Citizens Committee for Law and Order in Westchester County informed the public that it had invited an organization called People's Artists to conduct, as reported in the *Daily Worker* on August 2, 1949, another concert program "in defiance of the fascist gangs, which have been intimidating progressive residents of the community since the assault on the concert audience."

Paul announced at a Harlem protest rally that he would be going back to Peekskill. The date of his return would be Sunday, September 4, at 2 P.M. The site for the Sunday concert was to be one mile from Lakeland Acres, at the former Hollowbrook Country Club.

Numerous organizations pledged to defend the concert against any attack, including the International Fur & Leather Workers Union and the Bronx County American Labor Party.

Members of the Westchester Committee for Law and Order met in Albany with the assistant Counsel to the Governor and demanded a special investigator to supercede the Westchester District Attorney, who had been implicated in the violence of the first Robeson concert. Later, the CIO United Public Workers called on the Governor to remove Westchester officials and to demand prosecution of the "mobsters." Obviously, Labor Unions—the Bronx Jewish People's Fraternal Order, the Toms River, N.J., Federated Egg Producers Cooperative, to name a few—were behind Paul's right to sing. *The New York Times* also spoke out:

* * *

Mr. Robeson, whatever his other qualities, is one of this generation's most magnificent singers. . . . We defend his right to carry his art to whatever peaceably assembled groups of people he wishes.[14]

But Legionnaires and others who were against Robeson felt otherwise. Anti-Semitic and antiblack epithets were heard everywhere. These groups said they would have thirty thousand people on hand for the second concert and that they would parade outside the concert grounds.

Everyone—including the Legionnaires; also the majority of concertgoers who were not communists or radicals, but liberals from Harlem, Westchester, the Bronx, who came simply to hear a great artist sing; and the Westchester County Sheriff and the state police—knew there would be trouble on September 4. Paul and his friends hired guards and used volunteers, some 2,500 strong, to protect the crowds. On Sunday afternoon, these guards, along with state troopers amounting to an army and hundreds of Sheriff's deputies, were ready for riot.

Twenty-five thousand people came to hear Paul sing. Frantic efforts by the American Legion could muster no more than a thousand protesters. On the road facing the huge gully where the audience sat in a vast semicircle in front of the stage, the thousand Legionnaires marched back and forth. They were led by a drum and bugle corps from the Sing Sing Prison orchestra. They carried American flags and sang, "Roll out the Commies, we've got the Reds on the run." They also shouted anti-Jewish and antiblack abuse. As the audience continued to arrive by the thousands into the concert grounds, hundreds of men and women screamed epithets at them. This jeering throng lined the route along which Paul and the concertgoers had to pass.

The car in which Paul rode came slowly through the screaming crowd. Protected by guards, he strode purposefully into the concert area. But before he sang, others participated in the program. "The Star Spangled Banner" was rendered by Sylvia Kahn, who had been mauled in the attack at Lakeland Acres the week before. The balladeer Pete Seeger sang folk songs.

When Paul finally stepped up to the microphone, a roar began at the back of the audience and swept forward, cresting in an ovation of overwhelming applause. He stood on a platform beneath a tree, with his own guard surrounding him. And in a manner that had become by now characteristic, he cupped one hand over his ear. Overhead, a helicopter swooped down, trying to drown him out. But Paul did sing, his great, deep voice resounding through the valley as he began:

> *When Israel was in Egyptland,*
> *Let my people go!*
> *Oppressed so hard, they could not stand,*
> *Let my people go!*
>
> *Go down, Moses,*
> *Way down in Egyptland.*
> *Tell ole Pharaoh*
> *To let my people go.*

The audience roared its appreciation and succeeded in silencing the bugles and jeers from the Legionnaire groups. The applause was deafening, particularly when Paul sang his moving rendition of "Ol' Man River."

The program continued for another hour and a half. Throughout, Paul kept wondering how the day would end and what manner of violence would come with sundown. As he sang, his dark eyes wandered over the audience and held to it. A faint smiled played about his lips.

The enormous crowd sat enthralled. Many there were well known, controversial. There was the still figure of Benjamin Davis, lawyer and New York City

Councilman under indictment in the Smith Act conspiracy trial of the eleven Communists; and Robert Thompson, New York Communist Party leader. Shirley Graham, the writer who would later marry Dr. Du Bois, was there. And hundreds of union leaders and thousands of workers.

The concert ended at 4:30 P.M. in perfect order. The American Legion had failed in trying to stop Paul Robeson from singing. However, it did the next best thing. It commenced to attack the audience.

The stoning of the concertgoers began at the end of the concert when the enormous audience started to leave. The narrow exit from the grounds was quickly filled with Legion paraders. They attempted to push their way inside, but police managed to hold them back. The paraders then began stoning buses, which had to move at a crawl down the one exit road to New York. Every bus had its windows broken. Hundreds of cars came under attack. Men, women and children were hurt. One reporter's account of leaving the concert went like this:

> I came out in the car of [Ted Tinsley] who had his wife and one-year-old baby with him. Our car received characteristic treatment. It ran a gantlet down the state highway and was struck five times, shattering every pane in the car. One rock crashed through and struck a woman passenger in the car. [Tinsley's] baby was cut by the glass and her face was bleeding. As we rushed to a doctor I saw scores of cars that had similar marks.
>
> The cars are still coming out of the grounds as this is being telephoned.[15]

Mobs from surrounding communities spread out for several miles along the exit road. If a car or bus made it safely away from the concert grounds, it was caught out in the open farther down the line. A New York *Daily News* photographer snapped a picture of Eugene Bullard, first black aviator of World War I, as he was being attacked by state troopers, a policeman and a deputy sheriff.

A black reporter wrote in *New York Age:* "I still smell the sickening odor of blood flowing from freshly-opened wounds, gasoline fumes from autos and buses valiantly trying to carry their loads of human targets out of range of bricks, bottles, stones and sticks."[16]

The chaos—the noise of motor cars, screaming women, the sickening *whonk* of billy clubs and stones, was an ugly commentary on America at its worst. Hundreds of miles away in the South, white bigots set up flaming crosses protesting communism and black hero Robeson. Paul was burned in effigy from a tree.

"The Peekskill Riot," as it quickly became known, flashed in photographs around the world. Thousands of words were written about it. A rash of articles tried to dismiss the violence and racial overtones, saying that the Communists had created the whole affair. Concertgoers who had risked their lives to uphold their belief in free speech and freedom of assembly were depicted as rabble-rousing Reds. Still, the voice of reason and deep concern could be heard.

The *Christian Century* published an article that September entitled, "Peekskill Shadow," in which it erroneously reported that those who threw stones were teenagers. But the article did say that "Democrazy is . . . well what is it? Democracy is a lot of things and among them not the least is self-discipline and respect for the right of a minority peaceably to assemble and to express its views."

Paul felt completely shattered by his Peekskill experience. Tears rolled down his face as he talked to reporters after the riot. The hate he had seen was appalling. But he was so thankful that these many thousands had come bravely to hear him sing.

Perhaps the power of his voice was the most he could hope to give to his country in these troubled times. There were some who would even deny him the right to sing.

"I will sing," he said, "whenever the people want to hear me. I sing of peace and freedom and of life!"[17]

Paul was weary, tired to his very soul of the clamor against him. And although he still possessed his magnificent voice, freedom for himself, for his people, seemed far out of reach.

The "shadow" of Peekskill had passed but the specter of abuse followed Paul wherever he went. He was vilified in newspapers across the nation and accused of fomenting the riot himself. Well-known, conservative columnists wrote such statements as: "Only one who suffers from race prejudice can forgive Paul Robeson his numerous indecencies, which would never have been tolerated in a white man. . . ."[1] And: "Paul Robeson, spoiled by years of flattery and social toleration by white debauchers . . ."[2]

Yet he continued to act upon what he believed to be right. On September 21, he was called to testify as a defense witness at the trial of eleven Communists. However, Federal Judge Harold R. Medina ruled irrelevant almost every question asked by the defense counsel.

The defendants were being tried for criminal conspiracy to teach and advocate force and violence to overthrow the United States Government. George W. Crockett, Jr., of the defense counsel asked Paul a series of questions designed to bring out the fact that Paul had heard the defendants make many speeches but had never heard them advocate violent revolution. But this Judge Medina would not permit:

Judge Medina to Crockett:

A series of questions such as you have been asking are bound to convey the impression that the facts stated in the questions are true, despite the fact that I ruled them out and despite the fact that it is obvious from my rulings that if asked and objected to I would sustain the objections and rule them out. I don't think that is what a lawyer should do. . . .[3]

Paul Robeson began addressing the court: "May I—

Judge Medina:

No, Mr. Robeson, I don't want to hear any statement from you. I can't find from anything in these questions that you have any knowledge of the facts that are relevant in this case.[3]

Perhaps Paul was ahead of his time, in knowing what he believed to be true; and as a lawyer, himself, in knowing that the evidence he had to give, indicating no conspiracy, was indeed relevant.

Eight years later, in 1957, the Supreme Court would establish this fact in another case. Fourteen Communists were under a similar indictment. In the 1957 case, the Supreme Court held that the defendants had been found guilty by a lower court *even though* the evidence given revealed no conspiracy to overthrow the government by force and violence.

Paul continued to express his belief in the constitutional right of free speech and assembly. But now more than ever, a large portion of the white community feared him. Intimidation had been used in order to try to stop owners of an arena in Los Angeles from allowing him to give a concert there. And even though the Los Angeles City Council banned the concert, sixteen thousand people turned out to hear him.

On he went on his tour around the country, giving concerts in Ohio, Illinois and Pennsylvania. Wherever he went there was tension and harassment; yet there was never another Peekskill. But the strain of contemplating what might well happen at any time further exhausted him. Indeed, Paul seemed to age visibly.

But what kept him going was that his own black people turned out to hear him in triumphant numbers. No one could doubt that he was theirs and they were his. And nothing so divided black and white America for and against him more than this single fact.

By late fall, this towering man who had been followed by reporters the world over was hardly mentioned anymore in important segments of the white press, even though he made numerous public appearances. His records suddenly could not be found anywhere in America. It is a fact that 1949 would be the last year for a decade that he would sing in the large halls and auditoriums of the American concert circuit. The majority of black people stayed spiritually at his side, although by now they believed he meant to lead them into the radical political movement. That part of him they generally ignored. He may have desired to bring them to a deeper understanding of radical politics, but certainly not for the benefit of Communists; rather, for their own black advancement, for the raising of their consciousness to a world view of darker peoples. He believed that only radical politics would give blacks freedom to undo age-old grievances.

For the majority of blacks, Paul remained their star and their "soulful" leader as the great Dr. W.E.B. Du Bois remained their intellectual one.

He was one of the principal speakers at a Harlem celebration for one of the Communist eleven, Benjamin Davis, when Davis was set free on $20,000 bail. The outdoor rally was held at Lenox Avenue and 111th Street. Paul said he was glad Ben Davis was released and urged that he be re-elected to the City Council. Later, there was a motorcade with hundreds following on foot, carrying red light torches. Some incident occurred. Police and bystanders alike were injured, as empty bottles, bricks, tin cans rained down from windows and rooftops along the avenue. Simply one more unfortunate incident in the turmoil that followed Paul wherever he went.

Walter White, Executive Secretary of the NAACP, wrote in the spring of 1950:

> I have been nauseated and saddened at seeing him [Paul] fawned upon and shamelessly used by the lunatic fringe of [Communist] party-liners whose mental and moral characters were such as to make them unworthy to shine the shoes of so decent and courageous a man as he. It is because I have known him so long and well that, sharing as I do his criticism of white hypocrisy and the glaring weaknesses of democracy as they are manifested in bigotry and colonialism, I believe him in grievous error in his thinking that Communism of today's Soviet Russia offers the way out for Negroes and other exploited minorities.[4]

Mr. White expressed the utter disappointment in Paul felt by many in the black leadership. Yet Paul's revolt was a deep spiritual revulsion during twenty-five years of his life in America. He knew that his country misunderstood its nonwhites and those of the world at large most of all. Therefore, it did grave damage to its nonwhite peoples and those of the rest of the world as well.

In May, the director of the Rutgers University Press, Earl Schenck Miers, wrote about Paul in *The Nation* in a sensitive and just appraisal:

> Any appraisal of Robeson must begin with the fact that he represents both the exception to average human experience and its rule. His success as an artist has made him a citizen of the world and set him apart from the masses, both white and black. He has a remarkable mind and such a gift for languages that he mastered Russian and Chinese more easily than the typical student can stumble through a freshman course in French or Spanish. But the emotional Robeson, the man living within his heart, is not really different from

other Americans who have sprung from a similar environment and experienced similar frustrations, and whose spirits show the results of day-by-day chafing in the scar tissue of lasting resentment. As a product of his times Robeson today is perhaps more all-American than he was as a member of his college football team.[5]

Herein lies the key to Paul and to the kind of man he had always been. His lasting resentment; his inability to accept the fact that he could sing in the finest concert halls in the land and yet be forced to ride in the freight elevator around the corner; the fact that, having sung his heart out in some city in the hinterland of America, he could not even drink a glass of water at the drugstore on the corner because of his complexion. Because he was a citizen of the world, Paul could see such despicable local conditions in the broadest of lights. Never was he able to accept this evil, stupid discrimination.

Paul had publicly stated that he had never been a member of the Communist Party. But apparently, some members of the American government didn't believe him. By 1950, his every movement was being watched by the Federal Bureau of Investigation. FBI agents went wherever he went. They watched his home and tapped his phone lines, so Paul said.

However, there was a growing concern in important quarters of America over such invasion of privacy. On June 1, 1950, Senator Margaret Chase Smith of Maine, with six other Republican senators, signed a Declaration of Conscience which repudiated the kind of intimidation Paul and others were faced with. In her speech for the declaration she said:

> I think it is high time that we remembered that we have sworn to uphold and defend the Constitution. I think it is high time that we remembered that the Constitution, as amended, speaks not

only of the freedom of speech but also of trial by
jury instead of trial by accusation. . . .

The American people are sick and tired of
being afraid to speak their minds lest they be politically smeared as Communists or Fascists by
their opponents. Freedom of speech is not what it
used to be in America. It has been so abused by
some that it is not exercised by others. . . .

It is high time that we . . . started thinking
patriotically as Americans about national security
based on individual freedom. It is high time that
we all stopped being tools and victims of totalitarian techniques—techniques that, if continued
here unchecked, will surely end what we have
come to cherish as the American way of life.[6]

The government's willingness to fight communism
was put to the test when, on June 25, "North Korean
forces equipped with Soviet-made weapons"[7] invaded
South Korea. On the 27th, President Harry Truman
ordered American naval and air forces into Korea.
Clearly, a war had started which left small room at
home for the right of free speech and political toleration.

Early in July, Paul Robeson was the principal
speaker at a Harlem meeting sponsored by the Council on African Affairs and the Committee for a Democratic Far Eastern Policy, among others. He demanded in his speech that America leave "hands off
Korea," clearly an unpopular view at the time and
hardly distinguishable from the Communist Party line.
Yet it must be kept in mind that the phrase was spoken by a man exercising his right of free speech. Nevertheless, a month later, the Department of State canceled Paul's passport.

Paul refused to give up his passport. State and local
officials of the Immigration and Customs services and
the FBI were ordered to stop him if he attempted to
leave the country. Earlier in the year, he had made a

trip to the Soviet Union, and upon his return had praised the USSR and was said to have disparaged what was being done by the U.S. Government in Korea. This, said the State Department, was the reason his passport had been marked "null and void." The outbreak of war and the communist-hunting hysteria of the 1950's was cause enough for the government to refuse passport privileges to other radical thinkers and activists as well. In 1951, Dr. Du Bois and his wife, author Shirley Graham, had their passports canceled. They and Paul Robeson were confined to the United States for the next eight years.

The Council on African Affairs, of which Paul was chairman, lashed out at the State Department in an angry public statement:

> The invalidation of the passport of Paul Robeson . . . by the State Department is another blatant example of the administration's efforts to silence the demand of Negro Americans for their full rights as citizens and the demand of the American people generally for the preservation of world peace and protection of their dwindling democratic rights here at home.[8]

Very shortly after, the passports of Paul's wife, Essie, and that of his son, Pauli, were also canceled.

The Robeson family had committed no crime. Paul had spoken out loudly for what he believed. He had always advocated peace and friendship with the Soviet Union. But now his government thought peaceful coexistence with Communism impossible. It had joined politics inside the U.S. with foreign policy and believed that the extension of communism in Southeast Asia would bring political disaster to the party in power at home.

The harassment of a strong, sensitive man like Paul Robeson all during the 1950's, beginning with the passport ban, was hateful and absurd. In foreign countries, it was thought to be an evil, diabolical act.

This feeling was particularly strong in the developing countries where black, brown and yellow peoples were the majority. Trade unions and peace and revolutionary groups all sent messages of support for Paul and condemned the United States. In England, his friends worked to pressure the government to let him travel. Eleven members of Britain's Parliament led a movement to bring Paul to England; America received a bad press from New Delhi to Moscow. The attempt to silence and destroy him simply distorted the image of democracy in the rest of the world.

Since he was unable to leave the country, he couldn't give a series of concerts abroad as he had planned. He couldn't sing on the American concert stage or for Sunday musical societies, for art patrons no longer wanted him as their honored guest. He could perform for radical organizations, and the more he sang for these, the more his fellow Americans and government harrassed him.

Early in September 1950, the Madison Square Garden Corporation in New York refused to rent its mammoth facility to the Council on African Affairs for a meeting on September 14. The reason for the refusal was that the Council was listed by the Attorney General as a "subversive" organization. The meeting was to be a rally and a public protest against the revocation of Paul's passport. Since no hall could be found, Paul and his friends and associates took to the streets.

On September 9, some three hundred people rallied at 116th Street and Seventh Avenue. Ben Davis spoke, assailing the Internal Security Act (known as the McCarran Act) passed by Congress, which required all communist and Communist-front organizations to register with the Justice Department and to furnish its lists of their members. While membership in a communist organization was not to be considered unlawful, the Act did deny passports to Communists and denied them work in government or defense plants. Communists or so-called front groups could not broadcast over the radio or use the mails unless their messages were labeled "Communist-inspired."

Ben Davis said at the rally on 116th Street that the supporters of the bill might "find themselves in their own damned concentration camps soon."[9]

Paul spoke next, climbing effortlessly up on the sound truck, which was decorated with American flags. When he was ready, his deep, sonorous voice rolled out, solemn in its intensity. He was already "politely imprisoned," he said, and barred by the Department of State from doing his life's work. He "urged the Negro people to join their true friends"—as reported in the words of *The New York Times*, "the Communist Party"[9]—in the difficult task of preventing American intervention in Korea.

Still, on September 22, 1950, President Truman vetoed the Internal Security Act:

> There is no more fundamental axiom of American freedom than the familiar statement: In a free country, we punish men for the crimes they commit but never for the opinions they have. . . . We would betray our finest traditions if we attempted, as this bill would attempt, to curb the simple expression of opinion.[10]

The President's veto was overridden by Congress and the Internal Security Act of 1950 was put into effect on September 23, 1950.

The State Department had refused Paul his right to travel abroad because, it said, such travel would be contrary to the best interests of the United States. But clearly and unofficially, he was refused because U.S. security dictated denial of passports to so-called Communists and he refused to say any longer whether he was one.

Early in 1951, Paul filed suit in Washington Federal Court against Secretary of State Dean Acheson, to assert that political considerations had no part in any

American citizen's constitutional right to travel. The suit was dismissed and Paul couldn't appeal until August 1951. And in the summer, he would again apply for a passport only to have his application once again denied.

At the end of January 1952, he was scheduled to speak in Vancouver, British Columbia, Canada, at a meeting of the Mine, Mill and Smelter Workers Union. At Seattle, he was stopped by U.S. Immigration officers and informed that if he crossed the border, he would be subject to five years' imprisonment and a $10,000 fine. The law, the authorities told him, barred his departure in "the best interests of the Government."

It might have been to his own "best interests" if he had simply crossed the border and left America behind. But this, Paul would never do. For he knew he had a perfect right to travel and that his own government was attempting to strong-arm him into silence by keeping him in the country.

Government hounding continued for years and created a constant struggle for Paul. Had he been less of a man, with less secure belief in himself, he might have faltered and given up his integrity in the safety of silence. Instead, he chose to relinquish his six-figure annual income from records, concerts and speeches. The $2,000 or so a year he now made he sometimes gave away to organizations. This, to some Americans, was indeed a betrayal and a condemnation of the American dream and way of life.

Walter White wrote in *Ebony* magazine:

> But no honest American, white or Negro, can sit in judgment on a man like Robeson unless and until he has sacrificed time, talent, money and popularity in doing the utmost to root out the racial and economic evils which infuriate men like Robeson. He is an ominous portent to white democracy in the United States, Europe, the Union

of South Africa and Australia of what other colored men may turn to in frustration and despair.[11]

Still, he sang when and wherever he could. Again denied entry into Canada, he sang at the Peace Arch on the U.S.–Canadian border south of Vancouver, in May to some 40,000 people.

At the end of 1952, the Soviet Union awarded him its highest honor, the Stalin Peace Prize. But he was denied permission to travel to accept the award, which was then presented to him in New York by Soviet officials. It turned out that the $25,000 prize would prove hard to spend. The U.S. Government determined that the prize was for "services rendered" to the Soviet Union and therefore taxable.

I have been deprived of my livelihood [Paul said]. I have been stopped from functioning as an artist, which means that I have been denied the right to be a full human being. . . . How much longer will they imprison me? Ten more years? Even if they had put me on trial and found me guilty of something there would have been a limit to my term of imprisonment. I'd be free now.[12]

The next year, he and Essie sold their lovely home in Enfield, Connecticut. They needed the money, of course, and they no longer wished to live among people who no longer wanted them around. It hurt Essie, Paul said, for she loved the big house.

Petty punitive actions continued against Paul. He was no longer Walter Camp's All-American end for 1917 and 1918—his name had been removed from the *American Sports Annual*.

Throughout, he insisted on singing and he did sing, in parks, in school auditoriums and in black churches, where he had first lifted his voice in the sorrow songs of his people.

He continued his long, protracted passport suit

against the government. Each year, he reapplied for the passport. It was denied him in 1954 for travel to the Soviet Union, to attend Moscow's Soviet Writers' conference. Yet slowly, colored peoples over the world rallied to him. India asked the U.S. Government to give Paul his passport so he might visit there. The U.S. Government remained silent and the Indian and other governments began to wonder what America was afraid of.

Paul asked the State Department in 1955 to lift restrictions on his travel so he could give a concert for a union group in Vancouver, British Columbia. Furthermore, he asked for his passport so that he could accept engagements in Britain, India and the Soviet Union. On July 19, the State Department finally ruled that he could travel to and from Canada as often as he wished. But restrictions otherwise were still in effect. Although a Canadian concert series had been arranged, the Canadian government—perhaps fearing "guilt by association"—refused Paul entry into its country.

Again, Paul applied for a passport the same month, saying he was "a loyal, native-born American citizen." He asked the Federal District Court in Washington, D.C., to direct the State Department to grant him a passport. Naming Secretary of State John Foster Dulles as defendant, he further sued for a court order to allow him to visit Canada, Mexico and other western hemisphere countries not requiring a passport. The District Court held that Paul would have to file an affidavit showing that he was not a Communist. He refused and the passport was again denied.

Paul stood outside the Federal court building where his case had been heard. Television cameras were set up. When all was ready, he said he thought it absurd that Soviet farmers, as part of an agricultural exchange program, could visit the United States; that American Baptist preachers could go to Moscow; yet he, Paul Robeson, was "not allowed to travel because of my friendship—open, spoken friendship—for the

Soviet people and the peoples of all the world." Then, throwing back his head, he proudly spoke lines from *Othello*:

> I have done the state some service and they know 't. • • •
> I pray you, in your letters,
> When you shall these unlucky deeds relate,
> Speak of me as I am; nothing extenuate,
> Nor set down aught in malice.[13]

Paul sang in Russian and then parts of "Water Boy" in English to prove that he still had an exceptional voice, that he wished to travel in order to fulfill concert engagements. He was fifty-seven years old now. Still a strong, vigorous man, but it was difficult to tell whether his voice had deteriorated, he had used it so little in the past few years.

But he was constantly receiving invitations to sing and messages of concern and hope from all parts of the world. There was a standing invitation for him to appear in London in *Othello*. English friends launched a campaign to help him. A National Paul Robeson Committee was set up in Manchester to bring Paul to England and to request that his homeland allow him to come. Professors, union leaders, church leaders, members of Parliament, all joined the bipartisan committee. Paul sent a tape-recorded message and songs to repay the tribute shown him.

At home in the United States, there had been a slight shift away from the panicky retreat from democratic principles. During the time that Paul lost his position as most respected black man in America, other blacks had found it necessary to go along with the reactionary communist scare and suspicion of the foreign-born or else find themselves blacklisted and unable to work. The Truman Administration could show only narrow accomplishments in the area of equal rights. It had ended discrimination in the federal government and in the armed forces by executive order. It had raised the minimum wage, passed a public housing act and increased and extended social security benefits. But national health insurance, federal aid to education, sane and equal immigration laws and all-important civil rights legislation were all defeated by Congress.

Yet with the Supreme Court decision on school desegregation in 1954, it appeared that black Americans at least would finally receive some redress from hundreds of years of grievances.

But the hunt for "disloyal" Americans and communists continued:

> "Un-American activities" committees functioned without ever defining either "American" or "Un-American"; "loyalty" tests and oaths lacked any clear notion of what loyalty meant; elaborate "security" screenings sought to assure security by aimless inquiries into the private activities, beliefs, and intellectual interests of civil servants. A person's conduct, which since the Middle Ages had been considered the only proper test of loyalty or security, was now ignored in favor of inquests into a person's intentions, ideas, associations, and other tests so vague as to guarantee confusion and error.[14]

The House Un-American Activities Committee (HUAC) remained, holding hearings all through the 1950's.*

In 1956, Paul Robeson continued his ongoing passport suit against Secretary of State John Foster Dulles. Former Secretary of State Dean Acheson had first revoked Paul's passport in 1950 with the excuse that his travel abroad "would be contrary to the best interests of the United States." Mr. Dulles continued resisting

* HUAC's name was formally changed to Committee on Internal Security in February 1969, when its constitutionality was challenged for the first time by a ruling of a panel of three judges of the United States Court of Appeals for the Seventh Circuit, Chicago.

Paul's appeal for a new passport. Now, the government's position was that by refusing to swear the required non-Communist oath, Paul in effect had not completed his passport application. In June, the Federal Court of Appeals had refused unanimously to order the State Department to issue a passport to Paul. The Court stated he had failed to exhaust administrative remedies open to him, i.e., he had declined to execute an affidavit concerning past or present membership in the Communist Party.

This new decision was "based upon a narrow procedural ground" according to Paul's lawyer, and did not touch the fundamental problem of the constitutional right to travel and to a passport regardless of politics.

On June 12, a Subcommittee of the Committee on Un-American Activities convened at 10:00 A.M. in Washington, D.C., Chairman Francis E. Walter presiding. The hearing was one of a series being held on the "vital issue of the use of American passports as travel documents in furtherance of the objectives of the Communist conspiracy."[15]

Subpoenaed by HUAC, Paul Robeson was the witness. After the preliminaries of Paul's name, address and occupation, the Committee came to the heart of the matter:

MR. RICHARD ARENS [Director of Staff] to Paul Robeson: Are you now a member of the Communist Party?

MR. ROBESON: Oh please, please, please.

MR. GORDEN H. SCHERER [Representative from Ohio]: Please answer, will you, Mr. Robeson?

MR. ROBESON: What is the Communist Party? What do you mean by that?

MR. SCHERER: I ask that you direct the witness to answer the question.

MR. ROBESON: What do you mean by the Communist Party? As far as I know it is a legal party like the Republican Party and the Democratic Party. Do you mean—which, belonging to a party of

Communists or belonging to a party of people who have sacrificed for my people and for all Americans and workers, that they can live in dignity? Do you mean that party?

MR. ARENS: Are you now a member of the Communist Party?

MR. ROBESON: Would you like to come to the ballot box when I vote and take out the ballot and see?

MR. ARENS: Mr. Chairman, I respectfully suggest that the witness be ordered and directed to answer that question.

THE CHAIRMAN [Representative Francis E. Walter of Pennsylvania]: You are directed to answer the question.

(The witness consulted with his counsel.)

MR. ROBESON: I stand upon the fifth amendment of the American Constitution.

MR. ARENS: Do you mean you invoke the fifth amendment?

MR. ROBESON: I invoke the fifth amendment. . . .

MR. ARENS: Have you ever been known under the name of "John Thomas"?

MR. ROBESON: Oh, please, does somebody here want—are you suggesting—do you want me to be put up for perjury some place, "John Thomas." My name is Paul Robeson, and anything I have to say or stand for I have said in public all over the world, and that is why I am here today.

MR. SCHERER: I ask that you direct the witness to answer the question. He is making a speech. . . .

MR. ARENS: I put it to you as a fact, and ask you to affirm or deny the fact, that your Communist Party name was "John Thomas."

MR. ROBESON: I invoke the fifth amendment. This is really ridiculous. . . .

MR. ARENS: Do you know a woman by the name of Louise Bransten?

(The witness consulted with his counsel.)

MR. ROBESON: I invoke the fifth amendment.

MR. ARENS: I put it to you as a fact, and ask you

to affirm or deny the fact, that on February 23, 1945, you attended a meeting in the home of Louise Bransten, at which were present Max Yergan, Frederick Thompson, David Jenkins, Nancy Pittman, Dr. Lena Halpern, and Larry Fanning?

MR. ROBESON: I invoke the fifth amendment.

MR. ARENS: Do you know any of those individuals whose names I have just recited?

MR. ROBESON: I invoke the fifth amendment.

MR. ARENS: Who are Mr. and Mrs. Vladimir P. Mikheev? Do you know them?

MR. ROBESON: I have not the slightest idea but I invoke the fifth amendment. . . .

MR. ARENS: Have you ever had contact with a man by the name of Gregory Kheif[e]ts?

MR. ROBESON: I invoke the fifth amendment.

MR. ARENS: Now, Gregory Kheifets is identified with the Soviet espionage operations, is he not?

MR. ROBESON: Oh, gentlemen, I thought I was here about some passports.

Later in the hearing, Paul and Chairman Walters got into a mild argument concerning whether Paul was chairman of the Council on African Affairs. He refused to answer whether or not he knew Max Yergan and asked if such questions were legal:

THE CHAIRMAN: This is legal. This is not only legal but usual. By a unanimous vote, this Committee has been instructed to perform this very distasteful task.

MR. ROBESON: It is not distasteful. To whom am I talking?

THE CHAIRMAN: You are speaking to the chairman of this committee.

MR. ROBESON: Mr. Walter?

THE CHAIRMAN: Yes.

MR. ROBESON: The Pennsylvania Walter?

THE CHAIRMAN: That is right.

MR. ROBESON: Representative of the steelworkers?

THE CHAIRMAN: That is right.

MR. ROBESON: Of the coal mining workers and not United States Steel, by any chance? A great patriot.

THE CHAIRMAN: That is right.

MR. ROBESON: You are the author of all of the [immigration] bills that are going to keep all kinds of decent people out of the country.

THE CHAIRMAN: No, only your kind.

MR. ROBESON: Colored people like myself, from the West Indies and all kinds, and just the Teutonic Anglo-Saxon stock that you would let come in.

THE CHAIRMAN: We are trying to make it easier to get rid of your kind, too.

MR. ROBESON: You do not want any colored people to come in?

THE CHAIRMAN: Proceed.

Hereafter, the hearing took on a nightmarish quality. Paul attempted futilely to explain his great feeling for the Soviet people but it became clear that the Committee had already condemned him through "guilt by association":

MR. SCHERER: Why do you not stay in Russia?

MR. ROBESON: Because my father was a slave, and my people died to build this country, and I am going to stay here and have a part of it just like you. And no Fascist-minded people will drive me from it. Is that clear? I am for peace with the Soviet Union, and I am for peace with China, and I am not for peace or friendship with the Fascist Franco, and I am not for peace with Fascist Nazi Germans, and I am for peace with decent people in the world.

MR. SCHERER: The reason you are here is because you are promoting the Communist cause in this country.

MR. ROBESON: I am here because I am opposing the neo-Fascist cause which I see arising in these committees. You are like the Alien [and] Sedition Act, and Jefferson could be sitting here, and Frederick Douglas[s] could be sitting here, and Eugene Debs could be here.

THE CHAIRMAN: Are you going to answer the questions?

MR. ROBESON: I am answering them.

THE CHAIRMAN: What is your answer to this question?

MR. ROBESON: I have answered the question.

MR. ARENS: Did you send your son to a Soviet school in New York City?

MR. ROBESON: What is that?

MR. ARENS: Did you send your son to a Soviet school in New York City?

MR. ROBESON: I sent my son to a a Soviet school in the Soviet Union and in England, and he was not able to go to a Soviet school in New York.

MR. ARENS: I . . . invite your attention to this article. . . . Speaking of your son and his studies in a Soviet school in Soviet Russia: "Here he spent 3 years."

MR. ROBESON: And he suffered no prejudice like he would here in Washington.

MR. ARENS: "Then studied in a Soviet school in London."

MR. ROBESON: That is right.

MR. ARENS: "And in a Soviet school in New York."

MR. ROBESON: He was not able to.

MR. ARENS: Is that a mistake?

MR. ROBESON: That is a mistake.

MR. ARENS: That is a printer's error?

MR. ROBESON: And a wrong statement by me.

THE CHAIRMAN: Now, what prejudice are you talking about? You were graduated from Rutgers and you were graduated from the University of

Pennsylvania [sic]. I remember seeing you play football at Lehigh.

MR. ROBESON: We beat Lehigh.

THE CHAIRMAN: And we had a lot of trouble with you.

MR. ROBESON: That is right. . . .

THE CHAIRMAN: There was no prejudice against you. Why did you not send your son to Rutgers?

MR. ROBESON: Just a moment. It all depends a great deal. This is something that I challenge very deeply, and very sincerely, the fact that the success of a few Negroes, including myself or [baseball star] Jackie Robinson can make up—and here is a study from Columbia University—for $700 a year for thousands of Negro families in the South.* My father was a slave, and I have cousins who are share-croppers and I do not see my success in terms of myself. That is the reason, my own success has not meant what it should mean. I have sacrificed literally hundreds of thousands, if not millions, of dollars for what I believe in.

MR. ARENS: While you were in Moscow, did you make a speech lauding Stalin?

MR. ROBESON: I do not know.

MR. ARENS: Did you say in effect that Stalin was a great man and Stalin had done much for the Russian people, for all of the nations of the world, for all working people of the earth? Did you say something to that effect about Stalin when you were in Moscow?

MR. ROBESON: I cannot remember.

MR. ARENS: Do you have a recollection of praising Stalin?

MR. ROBESON: I can certainly know that I said a lot about Soviet people, fighting for the peoples of the earth.

MR. ARENS: Did you praise Stalin?

* Robeson is speaking here of a $700 average annual income per black family.

MR. ROBESON: I do not remember.

MR. ARENS: Have you recently changed your mind about Stalin?

MR. ROBESON: Whatever has happened to Stalin, gentlemen, is a question for the Soviet Union and I would not argue with a representative of the people who, in building America, wasted 60 to 100 million lives of my people, black people drawn from Africa on the plantations. You are responsible and your forebears for 60 million to 100 million black people dying in the slave ships and on the plantations, and don't you ask me about anybody, please.

MR. ARENS: I am glad you called our attention to that slave problem. While you were in Soviet Russia, did you ask them to show you the slave labor camps?

THE CHAIRMAN: You have been so greatly interested in slaves, I should think that you would want to see that.

MR. ROBESON: The slaves I see are still in a kind of semiserfdom. I am interested in the place I am, and in the country that can do something about it. As far as I know, about the slave camps, they were Fascist prisoners who had murdered millions of the Jewish people, and who would have wiped out millions of the Negro people, could they have gotten a hold of them. That is all I know about that.

MR. ARENS: Tell us whether or not you have changed your opinion in the recent past about Stalin.

MR. ROBESON: I have told you, Mister, that I would not discuss anything with the people who have murdered 60 million of my people, and I will not discuss Stalin with you.

MR. ARENS: You would not, of course, discuss with us the slave labor camps in Soviet Russia.

MR. ROBESON: I will discuss Stalin when I may be among the Russian people some day singing for them, and I will discuss it there. It is their problem.

MR. ARENS: I suppose you are still going to laud

Stalin like you did in 1949, or have your changed your appraisal?

MR. ROBESON: We will not discuss that here. It is very interesting, however, whether [it was because of] Stalin or the Soviet people, that from 1917 to 1947, in one generation, there could be a nation which equals the power of this one. . . . Nothing could be built more on slavery than this society, I assure you. . . .

MR. ARENS: While you were in Soviet Russia, did you make statements about your academic training in Marxism? Do you recall that?

MR. ROBESON: I do not recall that, but I have read a lot of Marx.

MR. ARENS: Do you know a woman by the name of Sheila Lind?

MR. ROBESON: I do not recall.

MR. ARENS: She wrote an article and I am going to lay it before you here so you can help me read it. This is the *Daily Worker*, 1949, in which she interviewed you and it tells about your achievements. Let me quote you this for the record and you can follow it here. She is quoting: " 'When I crossed the border from Poland into the Soviet Union,' he told me, 'It was like stepping into another planet.' "

MR. ROBESON: Exactly true, no more prejudice, and no more colored feeling, that is right.

MR. ARENS: " 'I felt the full dignity of being a human being for the first time.' "

MR. ROBESON: That is right, and that is still not here.

MR. ARENS: "He loved what he found there so much that, until the war, he returned to Russia for each new year."

MR. ROBESON: Every new year, and we took a little vodka.

MR. ARENS: "And he sent his son to school there. In Moscow he began to study Marxism."

MR. ROBESON: No. I started to study that in Enland, and all of my political education, strange to say, came in England where I lived and worked for many years and came back here. But my Marxist education . . . is in English background of the Labo[u]r Party. I went to Republican Spain with Lord At[t]lee to visit the At[t]lee Battalion, and I knew Sir Stafford Cripps, and I knew all of the members of the Labo[u]r Party, so you cannot blame that on the Russians. You will have to blame that on the English Labo[u]r Party. They have just invited me to come to London next week to sing to 140,000 miners up in Yorkshire. Do you think that you could let me go?

THE CHAIRMAN: We have nothing to do with that.

MR. ROBESON: Could you make a suggestion to the State Department that I be allowed to go?

THE CHAIRMAN: That would not do any good because the courts have ruled that it is not in the best interests of the United States to permit you to travel. . . .

MR. ARENS: In the summer of 1949 you came back to the United States, is that right?

MR. ROBESON: In the summer of 1949, yes, that is right.

MR. ARENS: And when you came back, did you make a speech in New York City, addressing a rally there? Do you recall that?

MR. ROBESON: I do not.

MR. ARENS: Let me quote from an article appearing in a paper, and see if you recall this speech: "I have the greatest contempt for the democratic press, and there is something within me which keeps me from breaking your cameras over your heads." Did you say that to the press people in New York City about the time you were addressing this rally in June of 1949?

MR. ROBESON: It is sort of out of context.

MR. ARENS: That was out of context?

MR. ROBESON: I am afraid it is.

MR. ARENS: Would you want to refresh your recollection by looking at the article?

Mr. Robeson: Yes. That was not at a meeting. Why do you not say what it was? When my son married the woman of his choice, some very wild press men were there to make a sensation out of it, and this thing was at his wedding, and I did not say "democratic press," I said "a certain kind of press," and I was reaching for a camera to break it, you are quite right.

Mr. Arens: That was a misquotation?

Mr. Robeson: It was not at a meeting. It was when I came out of my son's wedding, and why do you not be honest about this? There is nothing about a meeting, it was a wedding of my son.

Mr. Arens: Does not this article say, "Paul Robeson Addressing a Welcome Home Rally"?

Mr. Robeson: I do not care what it says. . . .

Mr. Arens: Do you know Ben Davis?

Mr. Robeson: One of my dearest friends, one of the finest Americans you can imagine, born of a fine family, who went to Amherst and was a great man.

The Chairman: The answer is "Yes"?

Mr. Robeson: And a very great friend and nothing could make me prouder than to know him.

The Chairman: That answers the question.

Mr. Arens: Did I understand you to laud his patriotism?

Mr. Robeson: I say that he is as patriotic an American as there can be, and you gentlemen belong with the Alien and Sedition Acts, and you are the nonpatriots, and you are the un-Americans and you ought to be ashamed of yourselves.

The Chairman: Just a minute, the hearing is now adjourned.

Mr. Robeson: I should think it would be.

The Chairman: I have endured all of this that I can.

Mr. Robeson: Can I read my statement?

The Chairman: No, you cannot read it. The meeting is adjourned.

Mr. Robeson: I think it should be and you should adjourn this forever, that is what I would say.[16]

Paul's appearance before HUAC did not end in a contempt of Congress citation or a jail sentence for him as it had for so many others. The Committee had not proved he was a Communist or that he was a threat and danger to American internal security. But what it had shown conclusively was that a strong man willing and able to face the consequences of his actions could not be intimidated.

By September, Paul had requested that the Supreme Court intervene in his passport controversy with the State Department. In November, the Supreme Court rejected his appeal, thus upholding the lower court's ruling.

But pressure continued on the U.S. Government to let him out of the country. *Pravda*, the Soviet newspaper, and Soviet radio broadcast a message of greeting from him in January of 1957. In his message, Paul said:

> The Negro people want a better life and deliverance from the forces of evil in the South of our country. Many consider it necessary to flee from there, as in former days of subjugation and slavery, but my people are showing unflinching courage, and the day will dawn when Negroes will be fully fledged citizens.[17]

Actors' Equity in Britain urged the Equity Council "to make representations in whatever quarters may have influence in allowing him [Robeson] to perform." That was in April. In May, Paul sang to his friends in England by transatlantic telephone. He sang in a New York studio for twenty minutes, ending his program with "Ol' Man River," again changing the words to "I must keep fightin' until I'm dyin'.'" Reports of the thunderous applause on the other side of the ocean had the effect of making the United States

Government look like an aging comic with pie on his face.

The October 1957 issue of *Ebony* magazine ran an article on Paul by reporter Carl T. Rowan. Entitled, "Has Paul Robeson Betrayed The Negro?" its editorial comment above the title read:

> The Robeson story has never been fully told. We believe that any American, no matter to what degree the public has pre-judged the case against him, ought to be able to get his story before the public. This is the reason why we are publishing this story and why Carl Rowan was willing to write it. . . .

Ebony was one of the few national magazines still interested in Paul and went about interviewing him in all seriousness. Rowan wrote:

> Today, he is a tragic figure, regarded by some as a casualty in the Cold War, viewed by others as the white man's biggest sacrifice on the altar of racial segregation, described by himself as a martyr, the victim of naive, cowardly Negro leaders who failed to display courage and back what Robeson refers to as his "struggle for my people."
>
> Whatever the reasons, for all practical purposes Paul Robeson's voice is silent today. The great concert impresarios pretend he no longer exists. City officials padlock public halls at the mere rumor that he is coming. Hollywood wouldn't touch him with a long-armed geiger counter. Ambitious Negroes shrink guiltily at the mention of his name. Autograph seekers who once trailed his every step have dropped by the wayside to make room for FBI agents. The Rutgers "old grads" who once fell over each other to offer social invitations when he performed in their town now curse his name and demand that it be stripped from the university's hall of fame. Newspapers

that once carried rave notices of his magnificent talents now run only an occasional item such as the following: "Danish dairy farmers have discovered American jazz increases the output of their cows as much as thirty per cent. But they say that the cows refuse to give as much milk when Soviet anthems sung by Paul Robeson were played for them."[18]

Mr. Rowan's article was generally sympathetic to Paul without sacrificing its objectivity. In his interview for this article, Paul was the first black man in recent memory to use the term "black power." Ten years later, the expression would spark the pride and will of a young and new black generation. He said, in part:

I think a good deal in terms of the power of black people in the world. . . . Now that doesn't mean I'm going back to Africa, but spiritually I've been a part of Africa for a long time.

Yes, this *black power* moves me. Look at Jamaica. In a few years the white minority will be there on the sufferance of black men. If they're nice, decent fellows they can stay. [Emphasis added by author.]

Trapped in semi-obscurity in his own country, the great Robeson did not die, nor did he fade away. He continued, living, speaking out whenever black publications cared to interview him, and practicing always for the time when he would be able to sing again in the concert halls of the world.

"The truth is," said a State Department spokesman, "that many foreign governments have notified us that they don't want him. We gave him permission to go to Canada but the government wouldn't let him in."

Paul answered: "They can keep me from going overseas but they can't keep news of Emmett Till and Autherine Lucy from going over." (Emmett Till, a black youth, was kidnaped and lynched at the town of Money, Mississippi, in the summer of 1955. In 1956, Autherine Lucy, also black, was admitted to the University of Alabama by Federal court order, but when mob violence occurred was barred by University officials.)

When a man is rich and famous, the world is open to him. He can go where he pleases, see all there is to see, possess all that money can buy; and he becomes dizzy with wonderment at the complete fulfillment of his expectations. But if he is rich and famous but born black, then the American Dream remains tantalizingly out of reach. Invisible doors clang shut before him and behind him. Dignity and respect are his only so long as he is careful never to overstep invisible racial barriers capriciously devised in the most unlikely places. Add to this the man's unpopular political beliefs and the situation of Paul Robeson in America becomes clear.

Robeson never worried about being careful, for he believed himself a citizen with the same rights as other citizens. He found it impossible to accept the situation of millions of his black people who would never know safety, a decent income, respect and dignity in their homeland. But never would he cease fighting for the cause of their freedom.

"Nobody can say that I betrayed the Negro," he told Carl Rowan in 1957. "Everything I did I did for the Negro, for the cause of his dignity and self respect."

Many blacks certainly believed that Paul had betrayed them and that he could bring only harm to the black cause. His name associated with any civil rights movement or organization would surely bring them accusations of "commie" or "red."

However, the Supreme Court's landmark 1954 decision on school desegregation brought new hope—as well as fear of turmoil following a great victory. Roy Wilkins, Executive Secretary of the NAACP, spoke to the Association's forty-sixth convention in 1955:

> Our great Association which has carried the fight thus far is faced with new challenges, new responsibilities, new and more pressing calls to duty, to devotion, intelligence and skill. Each and every officer and member, wherever he may be, shares the heavy burden of transition. None may shirk his duty, for that would be to betray the ones who come after. Let no one in tomorrow's world be able to say that in the years of decision, when destiny was in our hands, we failed to measure up.[1]

For twenty years Paul Robeson had been saying the same. And now there emerged blacks who were successful in turning their beliefs into deeds of action. In 1955 and 1956 in Montgomery, Alabama, a vitally important leader of black people forged a new civil rights movement. Believing in nonviolence as not only a tactic but a philosophy of life, he was Dr. Martin Luther King, Jr., who became the most articulate and persuasive black man in the era of desegregation:

> Many white men in the South see themselves as a fearful minority in an ocean of black men. . . . They look upon any effort at equality as leading to "mongrelization." They are convinced that racial equality is a communist idea and that those who ask for it are subversive.[2]

In the spring of 1958, Paul Robeson was sixty years old. A has-been to many, an old man now to others, he had for more than a decade been called a communist and "subversive." But slowly, the climate in America had changed. The black-led civil rights revolution had brought about the most significant gains for black people and the nation since the adoption, nearly a century earlier, of the Thirteenth, Fourteenth and Fifteenth Amendments to the Constitution. And these gains were sanctioned by the Supreme Court in a number of decisions that were designed to end discrimination in interstate transportation and public housing and require black participation on juries.

President Dwight Eisenhower, elected in 1952, formed an administration that by 1958 was known for its moderation in domestic affairs. Congress passed two civil rights bills in which the political rights of blacks were further guaranteed by the government; the minimum wage was raised to a dollar an hour and some nine hundred million dollars were provided for student loans. However, the Eisenhower Administration enlarged its Cold War loyalty system to include all agencies of government. It discharged employees seemingly at will and without specific charges of subversion, but in the "best interests of national security."

Somewhat reflecting the moderation of the administration, the Supreme Court did not show as clear a position on individual civil liberties as it had on civil rights. When Paul Robeson sued for his passport again in 1958, the whole travel problem was before the Court in two major passport cases. Now the State Department's power of restraint over Americans traveling outside the country was being seriously challenged. Indeed, in April of 1958, Paul was allowed "hemisphere travel," which meant he was free to travel in the western hemisphere where no passport was required. Nonetheless, he was unable to go to Europe or anywhere else overseas because he couldn't obtain a passport.

The pressure on the U.S. Government to let Paul travel in and out of the country steadily increased, however. African nations, the Soviet Union, India, China, England—all hoped to force America to lift travel restrictions on Paul so that they might honor him with celebrations for his sixtieth birthday. A year earlier he had been asked by a reporter if he would ever again pursue a concert career. Paul said that he wasn't sure, that his work as always would be based on the struggle of working people against those who oppressed them. That fall, he had given successful concerts on the West Coast to full houses. Nothing about him had changed, neither his militant racial views nor his politics. But perhaps Americans had changed; they seemed willing to accept his form of art without rejecting him totally.

Clearly, times had changed when in May 1958 he gave a recital at Carnegie Hall, his first such concert in a decade. The concert was sold out and he was given a standing ovation. The *Pittsburgh Courier* commented that "The . . . career of singer Paul Robeson has become a matter of international interest in recent months as the famed singer has re-entered the field of public entertainment."[3]

Paul was back and concert halls were soon clamoring for him again, the same ones that had so cruelly rejected him in the past. The deep, stirring voice was not quite as smooth as it once was but who would have expected it to be? It was still the greatest baritone voice of the time. And the drama of his bold and glowing personality made it throb and beat more richly in stunning presentations.

In June, the Supreme Court finally came to Paul's aid, ruling that the State Department had no right under law to deny a passport because of a man's "beliefs and associations." Thus, the passport office gave him the right to travel abroad. The next month, he left the United States for Europe.

The English hailed him with warmth and love. By July 1958, he was in London, where he intended to make his new home. Critics said his voice appeared even better at sixty than it had been at fifty. It was strong and vigorous, and all of his concerts—at Albert Hall, at the Palladium—were packed to capacity. Paul sang on television, and was the first black man to sing at St. Paul's Cathedral. Each program, sung in many languages, brought together folk music from around the world. Paul had such ease and naturalness on the stage. Graciously, he interrupted his singing to discuss the pentatonic scale and the history of black spirituals. His audiences were the students and he the professor. They would lean forward eagerly to learn all he had to teach.

Paul launched a concert tour outside of England. And by the next year, 1959, he was again an honored guest in his beloved Moscow. Premier Nikita S. Khrushchev welcomed in the New Year at the traditional Kremlin Ball; Paul participated in the musical program which was part of the Ball. Unfortunately, his crowded schedule of tours had taken its toll. It was not his voice that would break down, it was his health. A month after the Kremlin Ball, he was in the Kremlin Hospital suffering from bronchitis and fatigue. It was difficult for anyone to believe that he would interrupt his intensely busy life to lie in a hospital bed. He recovered quickly but his doctors were cautious concerning his health, saying he would have to have a period of rest and convalescence. Essie Robeson was also in the same hospital, undergoing treatment for an unspecified illness.

The hospital where the Robesons recuperated was reserved for Soviet Government officials and distinguished foreign guests. Paul was deeply loved by Soviet leaders as well as the people. The press wrote article after article about him. He appeared on television, looking strong, happy but a bit tired. He sang over the radio and visited Premier Khrushchev at his home. If he and Essie wished to stay in the Soviet Union forever, they were most wecome. For he had become the people's hero in a way he would never be in America.

The USSR had changed as had the rest of the world. Since 1945, the Soviet Union had become a great power with an organized way of life. Its military occupation armies in Central and Eastern Europe at the end of the war had helped to establish native revolutionaries in new Communist governments in country after country. The new "people's republics" set up constitutions similar to that established in the Soviet Union in 1936. Leaders of opposition political parties found it necessary to flee their countries or be silenced. A new Communist International was created in 1947. Called the Cominform, or Communist Information Bureau, it coordinated the policies of the "people's republics" along Soviet lines and was the propaganda center of the Cold War against the West.

By the 1950's the Soviet Union had recovered spectacularly from World War II. Joseph Stalin, Premier for thirty years, had successfully extended Communism in the postwar world. The spread of international communism had frightened America into extremely inflexible positions concerning internal security all through the 1950's. However, Joseph Stalin died in 1953. Nikita Khrushchev and Nikolai Bulganin became the top leaders in the Soviet Union in the middle 1950's. With them came a distinct softening of Stalin's suspicions of the West.

Yet the great Soviet experiment of communism, which was to have saved the workers of the world from exploitation, had come out completely wrong. As Eric Bentley wrote:

> Stalin had *more logical* concentration camps than Hitler, or so it could be claimed for a time and up to a point: in the end they were so far beyond all logic that the act of comparison becomes surrealistic, ludicrous—and inhuman. . . . The Russian disaster would be many times worse than the German because it is more than a disaster, it is also a tragedy, the greatest historical tragedy of the past hundred years, because, beyond all the physical suffering, it represented the desolating disappointment of the great hope of our era: the hope of Socialist humanism, the hope, to put it modestly, of a society which, through Socialism, shall be less oppressed, less insecure, less miserable.[4]

* * *

If Paul Robeson had become bewildered by the regime of Joseph Stalin or the outcome of the Soviet experiment, he would not say so publicly. In testimony before HUAC in 1956, he had said he would discuss Stalin with Russian people—"It is their problem." Essentially, his lasting regard for the Soviet Union can best be described as a deep love and admiration for the Russian people who had always loved and admired him in return.

For the next few years, Paul was in and out of hospitals suffering from a persistent circulatory illness and continuing bouts of fatigue. His health had indeed declined but he did find strength to play Othello in London. However, the old fire, the voice, had sadly at times become a shadow of its former strength. In another tour of Britain, he could still hold audiences in the palm of his hand, whether singing songs of the world or talking intimately of his grandchildren. There was no one quite like Robeson on stage; no one who could hold the attention of crowds with such down-to-earth conversation or poetry and fine renditions of folk music.

In Vienna, Austria, at the World Youth Festival, Paul attacked the United States, saying that its "foreign policy was being infiltrated by 'fascism.'" Americans, he said, could not "talk of giving full freedom and democracy to Africa when 18,000,000 of us do not have full freedom in the United States."[5] Forty American delegates walked out of the Festival because they were shouted down when they questioned Paul's statements. His statements revealed his continuing concern with problems of American blacks rather than any particular approval of the Soviet Union. His book, *Here I Stand*, had been published in 1958 by Othello Associates, New York. More than a biography, *Here I Stand* was a statement of principles and a commitment to black people and to the black American revolution. The black press reviewed the book favorably but the white press virtually ignored it. *The New*

York Times did not review it for another fifteen years. In the preface to a later Beacon Press paperback edition of the book, Lloyd L. Brown told of his query to the *Times* concerning the book. The Sunday Editor, Daniel Schwarz, replied:

> We have tried to find some record of what happened to Paul Robeson's book, *Here I Stand,* but our files do not go that far back. . . . I just want to assure you that we carefully consider every book we receive and I am certain that any book by Paul Robeson would not have been rejected for review if in the judgment of the editors it merited attention.[6]

And yet, in reviews from the rest of the world in 1958, *Here I Stand* merited considerable attention—from England to Japan. For it was the clearest, most well-written statement of beliefs Paul had ever given to the public:

> "How long, O Lord, how long?"—that ancient cry of the oppressed is often voiced these days in editorials in the Negro newspapers whose pages are filled with word-and-picture reports of outrages against our people. A photograph of a Negro being kicked by a white mobster brings the vicious blow crashing against the breast of the reader, and there are all the other horrible pictures—burning cross, beaten minister, bombed school, threatened children, mutilated man, imprisoned mother, barricaded family—which show what is going on.
>
> How long? The answer is: *As long as we permit it.* I say that Negro action can be decisive. I say that we ourselves have the power to end the terror and to win for ourselves peace and security throughout the land. The recognition of this fact will bring new vigor, boldness and determination

in planning our program of action and new militancy in winning its goals.[7]

In Budapest, Hungary, in 1959 Paul announced he would visit China despite the fact that his passport was "not valid" for China or Hungary. His passport expired in 1960; he was issued a new one but he never made the trip to China. He fell ill again and was placed in a Soviet hospital suffering from overwork and exhaustion. Doctors informed him that he must take more time for rest. But Paul always recovered enough to travel, and frequently he went from the USSR to London and back again and to East Berlin. Yet his health now seemed permanently broken. In October 1963, he entered a London nursing home, and in July, he left London for East Berlin where friends said he would "convalesce."

Le Figaro, a Paris newspaper, informed its readers that Paul had become disillusioned with communism. The London *Telegraph* reported it had received word that Paul Robeson would be " 'smuggled' . . . to a Soviet-bloc capital 'to keep him quiet' because he had 'broken with Moscow.' "[8] But the United States Embassy said it had no indication from Mr. Robeson that he had altered his political views.

A close friend of Paul's said the smuggling story was "sheer nonsense," which was probably true. Paul would simply have a checkup in East Berlin and then have a holiday at one of East Germany's famous and beautiful health spas. It turned out that his condition was such that he had to enter a nursing home again. Essie Robeson accompanied him to East Berlin and announced that he still suffered from a circulatory ailment.

The East German press service issued a statement from Paul, in which he pronounced the rumors of kidnaping and smuggling to be completely unfounded. He also sent a heartfelt message to his countrymen at home. The message was one of greeting and best wishes for the mammoth 1963 March on Washington.

The March, composed of Americans who cared deeply about civil rights, was to take place the following day. Paul knew that many of his old friends would be there; he might have wished he could be there, also.

On the eve of the March, one of his dearest friends, the old warrior himself, Dr. W.E.B. Du Bois, died of old age in far-off Ghana, Africa. The old order seemed to be passing at a moment in history when young blacks at home felt themselves most strong.

In the middle of September, Paul was yet again convalescing in a nursing home. Paul Robeson, Jr., had spoken to his father by telephone. He announced that his father had been suffering from exhaustion for several years but was much better now.

Three months later, it was announced somewhat suddenly that Paul Robeson, now sixty-six years old and in very poor health, would return to America. He hadn't sung in public since the autumn of 1961. Now his health was gone, and by all reports, his voice was gone as well. He would come home now to retire. *The New York Times* on December 20, 1963, ran a rather handsome photograph of Paul and an article which announced that Paul and Essie would be home on Monday. Essie described Paul as "still a sick man" and "very self-conscious about being thin."

The Robesons arrived two days before Christmas and were greeted at the airport by Paul, Jr., and his wife, Marilyn. The young Robesons were accompanied by their two children, who were now teenagers. So it was that the third and fourth generations of free Robesons in America welcomed home the second.

Paul's face was thin, old, behind thick glasses. There was an airlines tag attached to the button of his grey overcoat. There was something disquieting about the tag. It brought to mind the period of World War II, when immigrants from war-torn countries stood lined up across the length of huge train stations like the Chicago terminal. They had all worn identical tags attached to the buttons of wrinkled coats.

Paul Robeson smiled, hugged his son and daughter-

in-law, the children, and remained silent to reporters'
questions.

How did he feel coming back home after five years
and five months abroad?

Essie answered that he felt just fine. She said he
still felt that communism was "terrific" and that rumors to the contrary were absurd.

Then why were they returning?

Essie said, "It's Christmas—grandchildren and children."

As the Robesons left the airport, a moving incident
occurred. Many people, one a policeman, recognized
Paul, and without uttering a word, came quietly to
shake his hand.

So it was that the old fighter made it home to his
native land. He and Essie took a house on a quiet
street close to Harlem. Paul remained incognito with
an unlisted phone number. He saw few people and
lived quietly. And yet, around him blacks as well as
many whites would have honored him.

In the late 1950's, and in the sixties, young blacks
fought the long and difficult battle for their rights, as
he and their fathers had a generation before. Their
fathers had not given up their love for Paul. Seeing his
photograph in the newspapers again, they dusted off
the old records he had made, like the one called *King
Joe*, made in the 1930's, a salute to boxer Joe Louis,
the Brown Bomber. Paul had sung this "Joe Louis
Blues" to the accompaniment of Count Basie and his
orchestra. And another one, baritone with piano, "Nobody Knows de Trouble I've Seen," with Lawrence
Brown. And "Deep River" and "Hear, de Lam's A-
Cryin'." No matter that he was old now, his voice
gone. Were they not old as well?

They could still cherish his voice as they had formerly. And he was still one of their great ones, like
Dr. Du Bois.

Paul did make limited public appearances, as when
on April 22, 1965, he was made welcome at the New
York Hotel Americana on the occasion of the "*Free-*

domways Salute to Paul Robeson." *Freedomways*, a quarterly review "of the Negro Freedom Movement," was "the first national magazine to editorially welcome Mr. Robeson back to America (Feb. 1964)." And on the occasion of the "Salute to Paul Robeson," people flew into New York from all over the country. The Americana's Albert Hall was packed with old friends come to pay tribute to Paul and with young ones who were now learning about him.

Actor and playwright Ossie Davis was Master of Ceremonies. He told the eagerly waiting audience: "Our guest of honor has arrived in the hall and has been seated, so will the *real* Paul Robeson please stand."[9]

The real Robeson did stand as the spotlight fell on him. The real man, who, at the age of sixty-seven, still seemed to tower above everyone. The smile was warm, satisfied, as he shook hands with Ossie Davis. He spoke well that night and with ease, as was his way:

> I've never had a reception anything like this at any time that I can remember. . . . I would like for a moment to call your attention to an artist who has been closely associated with me in my career. I hope Larry is still here, my friend and colleague, Mr. Lawrence Brown, an authority on Negro and classical music who has been my partner in concerts for forty years. . . .
>
> The aspirations for a better life are similar indeed all over the world and when expressed in art, are universally understood. While we become aware of the great variety, we recognize the universality, the unity, the oneness of the many people in our contemporary world. In relation to this, on our travels we visited many peoples in Socialist countries. Today we know that hundreds of millions of people (a majority of the world's population) are living in Socialist countries or are moving in a Socialist direction. . . .

The large question as to which society is better for humanity is never settled by argument. The proof of the pudding is in the eating. *Let the various social systems compete with one another under conditions of peaceful coexistence, and the people can decide for themselves.*[10]

He had spoken like the humanist he had always been, and spoken with vigor and strength. But after several appearances in Los Angeles in the summer, poor health again overcame him, forcing him to retire completely.

In October 1965, Paul was found lying in a clump of weeds near Highbridge Park in Washington Heights, New York City. No one knew exactly what had happened to him. But Essie had reported Paul missing to the police at 12:45 A.M. Occasionally, she said, he lost his balance while suffering a dizzy spell. Perhaps that is what had occurred. Barely conscious, he was rushed to the hospital. At the Vanderbilt Clinic, he was found to have facial lacerations and injuries to his left ankle and right hip. His condition was listed as fair.

Paul recovered, but how quickly tragedy came to claim what was left of his happiness. In December, Essie fell seriously ill. It was not long before she died. Paul grieved for her, his wife and companion through the glory years and the years of trial. But he kept his pain and sorrow away from the eyes of the world, which seemed to watch and wait.

After Essie's death, Paul kept their home at 16 Jumel Terrace. Now, he saw only Pauli and Marilyn and their children in New York. Often, he spent time with his sister, Marion, who lived in Philadelphia. Infrequently, he made public appearances, as he did also in 1965 to honor the late Lorraine Hansberry, who had written *A Raisin in the Sun*. He attended the funeral of old friend Benjamin Davis, and was literally mobbed by well-wishers.

In 1967, at Rutgers University, there was growing

student criticism focusing on the fact that the picture of Paul was missing from the gallery of football players in the college gym. The Athletic Information Sports Director was quoted in the April 4, 1967, issue of the student newspaper *Targum,* saying, "We do not brag about him."[11]

Other campus papers then began a hue and cry over "the silent treatment accorded the most famous son of Rutgers." Finally, Paul's picture was put back in the Rutgers gym, but the fight for his full recognition continued.

Two years later, Paul lay gravely ill, suffering from a heart condition. His hospital room at University of Pennsylvania Hospital was reportedly closed by tight security to all but immediate family members. *Jet* magazine ran an article with a photograph of Paul:

> Throughout his glorious career, he suffered a heart condition of another kind—a broken heart, resulting from the refusal of the racist United States to accept him for the great actor and singer he was.[12]

Many said that the famed Robeson was not really ill, that going to the hospital was the only way he could keep away the hundreds who simply wished to see him now. However, he was seventy-one years old, and although far from done, he would not want accolades now for the past.

Nevertheless, honors came to him. In April of 1970, he was feted by the college that had pretended he did not exist for twenty years. At an affair sponsored by the Eastern Region of Alpha Phi Alpha Fraternity and the Rutgers Student Center, Paul Robeson, Jr., looking strikingly like his father, delivered a pointedly critical speech in Paul's place:

> This event today is significant because for many years those who run this country and most of the media have attempted to blot out the truth about

Paul Robeson. Even here at Rutgers, not so many years ago, Paul Robeson was an "unperson." His trophies were removed from the display case, and his name was unmentionable. . . .

Times have changed, but much of the truth still remains hidden, distorted and suppressed. The books you can buy in the bookstores, and the reference material you can find in most libraries either omit facts or falsify them. Newsreel footage on Paul Robeson in the United States has been confiscated and is not available even to educational TV stations.[13a]

Paul, Jr., went on to say that his father was not a "tragic misled figure, victimized by the times" as many persisted in saying:

Nothing could be further from the truth. Paul Robeson was way ahead of his time—a trailblazer. He knew full well the price he would have to pay and he paid it—unbowed and unflinching.[13b]

In November 1970, *Black World* ran an article entitled, "Paul Robeson: Black Star," by an old friend of Paul's, C.L.R. James. Mr. James's remarks were warm and nostalgic. They brought back memories of Paul's great achievements of earlier years. Blacks who read about Paul again felt a need to take out the old records and play them one more time.

What of the world—had it caught up with this extraordinary man, so way ahead of his time? For more than a generation Robeson had been advocating peaceful coexistence with Communist countries. And in 1971 it appeared that his own country had at last come around to his point of view. Since 1949, government administrations, whether Republican or Democrat, had steadfastly refused to "recognize" the Chinese Communist regime. But in July 1971, President Richard M. Nixon, one of the foremost anticommunists of the late 1940's and the 1950's, announced that he would go to Communist China, the first American president ever to do so.

And in August of that year, the U.S. Department of State revealed that it would no longer oppose Communist China's entry into the United Nations.

Furthermore, the Cold War between the Soviet Union and the United States seemed definitely to have thawed when in 1973 both superpowers signed agreements covering concerns ranging from oceanography to civil aviation. Henry Kissinger, then advisor to the President, was to say:

> We have China entering the world, the Soviet Union acting like a great power and less like a revolutionary, and the United States understanding she is no longer on a crusade. The leaders of these nations have learned the limits of previous policy. They now relate to each other in a constructive way; the tensions we see now are a healthy sign of growing. We are developing a code of conduct with our former adversaries and a system of competition with our friends.[14]

On a ten-day visit to the United States, Soviet Communist Party Leader Leonid Brezhnev spoke to the U.S. on television and then to a group of American businessmen on the subject of the Cold War:

> I ask you, gentlemen, as I ask myself, was this a good period? Did it serve the interest of the peoples? And my answer to that is no, no and again no.[15]

Moreover, after ten tragic years of military involvement in Southeast Asia, America concluded that it could no longer police the world. The country finally got out of the Vietnam War, only to discover that there was spectacular corruption in the Nixon government at home. Disastrous scandals in this "law-and-order" administration only began with the revelations of the break-in by the Committee to Re-Elect the President, at Democratic Party headquarters at Washington's Watergate building on June 17, 1972. The scandals spread like ocean waves, drowning high government officials in its path. Vice-President Spiro T. Agnew, in the era of government scandal, was forced to resign.

Such high-level misconduct and corruption not only astounded but horrified Americans and the rest of the world. In the light of them, it is an irony that twenty years before, in the 1950's, the U.S. feared that if it let Paul Robeson out of the country, he would embarrass it abroad.

The New York Times Book Review on October 21, 1973, reviewed Robeson's book, *Here I Stand*—exactly fifteen years after it was first published. In the same article, entitled "Paul Robeson Revisited," Professor Sterling Stuckey wrote:

> Robeson's fate illustrates the extent to which guardians of the culture are willing, when frightened, to attempt to blot from history a man's meaning, his very existence. If the real intent of the larger society's campaign against him was to terrorize Afro-America, then its purpose was achieved in full measure. . . .
>
> Until [Paul Robeson] is restored to his rightful place in the land of his birth, his treatment will represent in the future, as it has in the past, the single most striking example in our time of America's vulnerability on the question of human freedom.

By 1974, Paul Robeson was in full retirement. He lived quietly in Philadelphia with his sister, Marian Forsythe, keeping to his soul whatever was left of that gift he gave the world years before. On December 28, 1975, he suffered a stroke and was taken to Presbyterian Medical Center. Doctors there said he was ill with a severe cerebral vascular disorder. On January 23, he died at the age of seventy-seven.

Five thousand mourners attended Paul's funeral held at one of the oldest churches in America, Mother AME Zion Church at 151 W. 136th Street in Harlem, New York. It was at this church that Robeson performed when he was denied platforms elsewhere in America because of his political views. His last American concert was held at Mother AME Zion before he left the country after the travel ban against him was lifted.

The mahogany coffin had been opened for viewing for two days, but at the funeral, it was closed and draped by a blanket of red carnations on a bed of green ferns. Plans for Robeson's burial were not disclosed at the family's request.

During the service, Paul Robeson, Jr., spoke of his father as "a friend and as a great and gentle warrior with whom I worked and fought side by side."[16]

Tributes to Paul Robeson began soon after his death. The most recent took place at Avery Fisher Hall in New York. It was a fund-raising program for the Paul Robeson Archives, a non-profit organization at 157 W. 57th Street, New York, New York, for processing the 50,000 items concerning Mr. Robeson's rich and varied public life in the arts, and his unpublished writing. When processed, the material will be donated to the Moorland-Spingarn Research Center of Howard University in Washington, D.C. The Tribute celebrated Robeson's eightieth birthday with recollections of his career by friends and relatives.

The noted black actor, James Earl Jones, portrayed Mr. Robeson on Broadway in a one-man play entitled *Paul Robeson*, written by black playwright, Philip Hayes Dean. Its setting is an imaginary concert hall where Robeson, through the actor, Mr. Jones, exchanges dialogue with imaginary people across a span of years between his birth in 1898 and his death in 1976. *Paul Robeson* ran for 45 days at the Lunt-Fontanne Theatre after opening to mixed reviews. It was reopened in the spring of 1978 at the Booth Theatre by Joseph Papp, former head of the New York Shakespeare festival. Paul Robeson, Jr., called the play "a fictionalized and grossly distorted portrayal of Paul Robeson. It is my opinion that the script is a crude attempt to misrepresent my father . . . I am not associated with this project in any way."[17] Other charges that the play "was a pernicious perversion of the essence of Paul Robeson" were dismissed by Mr. Papp who said, "It's hard for a living legend to be treated on the stage. There's always someone who will say that is not the person."[18] Actually, Joseph Papp's support of the play was an expression of the feeling held by many that writers of plays and books should not be discouraged or censored from portraying black heroes.

Paul Robeson's reinstatement to a place of honor in American society continues, and it would seem, ever amid controversy. That reinstatement may never be complete. Yet his country no doubt owes him a position of esteem, for all the years it feared and punished him.

> Once he did not exist.
> But his voice was there, waiting.
>
> Light parted from darkness,
> day from night,
> earth from the primal waters.
>
> And the voice of Paul Robeson
> was divided from the silence. . . .[19]

So take out the old records again—"Honey," "Gloomy Sunday," "Nobody Knows de Trouble I've Seen." All should play the songs—one more time. Play "Ballad for Americans":

* * *

It will come again—our marching song will come again,
Simple as a hit tune, deep as our valleys
High as our mountains, strong as the people who made it. . . .

So it can never be said that nobody heard.

Notes to the Text by Chapter

CHAPTER ONE

1. *Christian Recorder*, June 18, 1891; W. S. Scarborough; in Herbert Aptheker, ed., *A Documentary History of the Negro People in the U.S.*, Vol. II, "Scarborough, 1891." Citadel Press, New York, 1964.
2. Paul Robeson, *Here I Stand*. Othello Associates, New York, 1958 (Reprint: Beacon Press, Boston, 1971, p. 11).
3. *Ibid.*, p. 15 (Beacon, p. 7).
4. *Ibid.*, p. 21 (Beacon, p. 13).
5. Similar versions of this exchange between father and son can be found in *The New Republic*, March 3, 1926, p. 42; and *Paul Robeson, Negro* by Eslanda Goode Robeson, pp. 19–20.
6. Paul Robeson, *Here I Stand*, p. 19 (Beacon, p. 16).

CHAPTER TWO

1. *The New York Times*, Sunday, January 16, 1944, Section 2, p. 1; Paul Robeson to Robert Van Gelder.
2. *Ibid.*
3. *New York Tribune*, a. November 25, 1917, Louis Lee Arms; b. October 28, 1917, Charles A. Taylor.
4. Paul Robeson, *Here I Stand*. Othello Associates, New York, 1958, p. 28 (Reprint: Beacon Press, Boston, 1971, p. 20).
5. Alexander Woollcott, *While Rome Burns*. The Viking Press, Inc., New York, p. 123.
6. Marie Seton, *Paul Robeson*. Dennis Dobson, London, 1958, p. 26.
7. Eslanda Goode Robeson, *Paul Robeson, Negro*. Harper & Bros., New York, 1930, pp. 76, 78.

CHAPTER THREE
1. Eslanda Goode Robeson, *Paul Robeson, Negro*. Harper & Bros., New York, 1930, p. 80.
2. *The New York Times*, April 20, 1925; p. 21.
3. Eslanda Robeson, *Paul Robeson, Negro*, pp. 110–111.
4. *Ibid.*, p. 112.
5. *The New York Times*, September 12, 1925; p. 9.
6. Avery Craven, Walter Johnson and F. Roger Dunn, *A Documentary History of the American People*. Ginn and Company, Boston, 1951, p. 681.
7. *The New Republic*, March 3, 1926; Elizabeth Sheply Sergeant, "The Man with his Home in a Rock: Paul Robeson" (pp. 40–44), p. 40.
8. Eslanda Robeson, *Paul Robeson, Negro*, pp. 136–137.
9. Gertrude Stein, *The Autobiography of Alice B. Toklas*, in Carl Van Vechten, ed., *Selected Writings of Gertrude Stein*. Random House, Inc., 1946 (pp. 3–208); p. 196.
10. Eslanda Robeson, *Paul Robeson, Negro*, p. 152.
11. *The New York Times*, May 18, 1930; Section 1, p. 31.

CHAPTER FOUR
1. *The New York Times*, May 22, 1930; p. 32.
2. *Ibid.*, September 14, 1930; Section 8, p. 2.
3. *The New Republic*, August 6, 1930; Stark Young, a review of *Paul Robeson, Negro*, by Eslanda Goode Robeson (pp. 345–346) p. 345.
4. Eslanda Goode Robeson, *Paul Robeson, Negro*. Harper & Bros., New York, 1930, p. 43.
5. *Ibid.*, p. 67.
6. *The New York Times*, December 19, 1930; p. 13.
7. Marie Seton, *Paul Robeson*. Dennis Dobson, London, 1958, p. 57.
8. London *Daily Herald*, July 11, 1930; W. R. Titterton.
9. Seton, *Paul Robeson*, p. 68.
10. *Ibid.*, p. 67.
11. *The Spectator*, June 15, 1934; Paul Robeson, "The Culture of the Negro."
12. New York *Amsterdam News*, October 5, 1935; T. R. Posten.

CHAPTER FIVE

1. R. R. Palmer, *A History of the Modern World*, Alfred A. Knopf, Inc., New York, 1957, p. 749.
2. Marie Seton, *Paul Robeson*. Dennis Dobson, London, 1958, p. 82.
3. *Ibid.*, p. 82.
4. *Ibid.*, p. 84.
5. *Ibid.*, pp. 94–95.
6. Palmer, *A History of the Modern World*, pp. 743–744.

CHAPTER SIX

1. *Pittsburgh Courier*, May 20, 1937; Louis Lautier.
2. London *Daily Worker*, November 22, 1937.
3. Federico Garcia Lorca, "The Ballad of the Spanish Civil Guard," March 1, 1938; translated by Langston Hughes; quoted in Joseph North, ed., *New Masses*, International Publishers Co., Inc., New York, 1969 (pp. 66–69); pp. 66–67.
4. *The American Century*, July 1939; Julia Dorn.

CHAPTER SEVEN

1. Earl Robinson and John LaTouche, "Ballad for Americans," RCA Victor Recording, sung by Paul Robeson with the American People's Chorus, 1939; as quoted in *Time* magazine, November 20, 1939, pp. 58–59.
2. Edwin P. Hoyt, *Paul Robeson: The American Othello*. The World Publishing Company, 1967, p. 106.

CHAPTER EIGHT

1. Chicago *Defender*, editorial, April 14, 1945.
2. Speech to New York *Herald Tribune* Forum, November 16, 1943. Quoted in N. Y. *Herald Tribune*, November 21, 1943, Section 8, p. 5.
3. *The New York Times*, April 12, 1944; p. 7.
4. These two quotes were gathered by the author from persons who wish to remain anonymous.
5. Stephen E. Ambrose, *Rise to Globalism*. Penguin Books, Inc., Baltimore, 1971, pp. 21–22.
6. Winston Churchill, "Iron Curtain" speech delivered at Fulton, Missouri, March 5, 1946; quoted in Barton J. Bernstein and Allen J. Matusow, eds., *The Truman Administration: A Documentary History*. Harper & Row, Publishers, Inc., New York, 1966 (pp. 215–219), p. 217.

7. Marie Seton, *Paul Robeson*. Dennis Dobson, London, 1958, p. 165.
8. *The New York Times*, November 26, 1945; p. 11.
9. *Ibid.*, September 24, 1946; p. 60.
10. *Ibid.*

CHAPTER NINE

1. Paul Robeson, *Here I Stand*. Othello Associates, New York, 1958, p. 47 (Reprint: Beacon Press, Boston, 1971, p. 39).
2. Edith Fowke and Joe Glazer, *Songs of Work and Freedom*. Roosevelt University, Chicago, Labor Ed. Div., 1960; "Joe Hill," p. 20.
3. *The New York Times*, May 7, 1947; p. 29.
4. *Ibid.*, October 8, 1946; p. 13.
5. President Truman's Address to Congress, March 17, 1948; in Barton J. Bernstein and Allen J. Matusow, eds., *The Truman Administration: A Documentary History*. Harper & Row, Publishers, Inc., New York, 1966 (pp. 269–271), p. 269.
6. Richard M. Freeland, *The Truman Doctrine and the Origins of McCarthyism*. Alfred A. Knopf, Inc., New York, 1972; p. 334.
7. *Ibid.*, p. 336.
8. Stefan Kanfer, *A Journal of the Plague Years*. Atheneum Publishers, New York, 1973, p. 140.

CHAPTER TEN

1. *I Vote My Conscience*: Debates, Speeches and Writings of Vito Marcantonio; Selected and ed. by Annette T. Rubinstein and Associates. The Vito Marcantonio Memorial, 1956, p. 261.
2. *Ibid.*
3. *The New York Times*, June 1, 1948; p. 1, cont'd p. 21, "Mundt–Nixon Foes Talk of Besieging Capital Tomorrow"; p. 21.
4. *The New York Times*, June 3, 1948; p. 1, cont'd p. 12, "Marchers Picket White House, Swarm In Capital"; p. 12.
5. Eric Bentley, ed., *Thirty Years of Treason*. The Viking Press, Inc., New York, 1973; "A Statement by John Howard Lawson" (pp. 161–165), pp. 162–163.
6. Walter LaFeber, *America, Russia, and the Cold War*,

1945–1971. John Wiley and Sons, Inc., New York, 1967, 1972, p. 73.

7. Barton J. Bernstein and Allen Matusow, eds., *The Truman Administration: A Documentary History.* Harper & Row, Publishers, Inc., New York, 1966, p. 104.

8. Marie Seton, *Paul Robeson.* Dennis Dobson, London, 1958, p. 194.

9. *The New York Times*, April 21, 1949; p. 6.

10. Robert Alan, *The Crisis.* "Paul Robeson—The Lost Shepherd"; Max Yergan quoted pp. 570–571.

11. *Ibid.,* Walter White, p. 571.

12. Seton, *Paul Robeson*, p. 196.

13. *Negro Digest*, March 1950; "Paul Robeson: Right or Wrong?" pp. 8–18; W.E.B. Du Bois, "Right," pp. 10–11.

14. *Ibid.,* Walter White, "Wrong," p. 14.

15. *Ibid.,* p. 18.

CHAPTER ELEVEN

1. Eric Bentley, ed., *Thirty Years of Treason.* The Viking Press, Inc., New York, 1973, pp. 768–769.

2. *Ibid.,* p. 769.

3. *The New York Times*, June 15, 1949; p. 6.

4. *Ibid.,* June 17, 1949; p. 3.

5. *Time* magazine, June 27, 1949, p. 36.

6. *Ibid.*

7. *Ibid.*

8. *Ebony* magazine, October 1957; Carl T. Rowan, "Has Paul Robeson Betrayed the Negro?" (pp. 30–42), p. 32.

9. Paul Robeson, *Here I Stand.* Othello Associates, New York, 1958 (Reprint: Beacon Press, Boston, 1971, p. 37).

10. *The New York Times*, July 18, 1949; p. 17.

11. *Commentary*, October 1950; James Rorty and Winifred Raushenbush, "The Lessons of the Peekskill Riots" (pp. 309–323), p. 313.

12. *Time* magazine, September 5, 1949; p. 15.

13. *Ibid.*

14. *The New York Times*, August 29, 1949; p. 16 (editorial).

15. *Daily Worker*, September 5, 1949; p. 9.

16. Marie Seton, *Paul Robeson*. Dennis Dobson, London, 1958, p. 213.
17. Howard Fast, *Peekskill, USA*. New York: Civil Rights Congress, 1951.

CHAPTER TWELVE

1. George Sokolsky, September 10, 1949, in syndicated column for Hearst Publications.
2. Westbrook Pegler, September 2, 1949, in syndicated column for Hearst Publications.
3. *The New York Times*, September 21, 1949; p. 18.
4. *Negro Digest*, March 1950; pp. 14–15.
5. *The Nation*, May 27, 1950; Earl Schenck Miers, "Paul Robeson—Made in America" (pp. 523–524), p. 523.
6. Barton J. Bernstein and Allen J. Matusow, eds., *The Truman Administration: A Documentary History*. Harper & Row, Publishers, Inc., New York, 1966; Margaret Chase Smith, "Republican Declaration of Conscience" (pp. 412–417), pp. 413, 414, 417.
7. Richard B. Morris, *Encyclopedia of American History*. Harper & Row, Publishers, Inc., New York, 1970, p. 398.
8. *The New York Times*, August 5, 1950; p. 16.
9. *Ibid.*, September 10, 1950; p. 47.
10. Bernstein and Matusow, eds., *The Truman Administration*, pp. 388–389.
11. *Ebony* magazine, February 1951; Walter White, "The Strange Case of Paul Robeson" (pp. 78–84), p. 84.
12. *Ibid.*, October 1957; Rowan, "Has Paul Robeson Betrayed the Negro?" pp. 32–33.
13. *The New York Times*, August 17, 1955; p. 14.
14. S. Morison, H. Commager & W. Leuchtenburg, *The Growth of the American Republic*, Vol. II. Sixth Edition. Oxford University Press, New York, 1969, p. 682.
15. Eric Bentley, ed., *Thirty Years of Treason*. The Viking Press, Inc., New York, 1973; Chairman Francis E. Walter, p. 770.
16. United States House of Representatives, Committee on Un-American Activities, *Hearings*. Subcommittee "Investigation of the Unauthorized Use of United States Passports—Part 3." Tuesday, June 12, 1956: "Testimony of Paul Robeson, Accompanied by Coun-

sel, Milton H. Friedman" (pp. 4492–4510), pp. 4494–98, 4504–09.

17. *The New York Times,* January 2, 1957; p. 6.
18. *Ebony* magazine, October 1957; Rowan, "Has Paul Robeson Betrayed the Negro?" p. 31.

CHAPTER THIRTEEN

1. F. Broderick, E. Rudwick and A. Meier, eds., *Black Protest Thought in the Twentieth Century. American* Heritage Series, The Bobbs-Merrill Co., Inc., 1971; Part II, "The Era of Legalism," p. 281.
2. *Ibid.,* Part III, "The Era of Non-Violent Direct Action"; "The Philosophy of Martin Luther King," p. 297.
3. *Pittsburgh Courier,* May 13, 1958.
4. Eric Bentley, ed., *Thirty Years of Treason.* The Viking Press, Inc., New York, 1973, p. 944.
5. *The New York Times,* August 4, 1959; p. 5.
6. Paul Robeson, *Here I Stand.* Beacon Press, Boston, 1971; preface by Lloyd I. Brown, p. xi.
7. *Ibid.,* Othello Associates, New York, 1958, p. 98 (Beacon, p. 90).
8. *The New York Times,* August 26, 1963; p. 2.
9. *Freedomways,* Vol. 5, No. 3; Summer 1965; p. 364.
10. *Ibid.,* excerpts from speech by Paul Robeson; pp. 373–375.
11. *Freedomways,* Vol. 9, No. 3; Summer 1969; George Fishman, "Paul Robeson's Student Days and the Fight Against Racism at Rutgers," p. 226.
12. *Jet* magazine, August 21, 1969; p. 10.
13. *Freedomways,* Vol. 10, No. 3; Summer 1970; Paul Robeson, Jr., "Rutgers Salutes Paul Robeson" (237–241); a. p. 237. b. p. 240.
14. *Time* magazine, July 30, 1973; p. 27.
15. *Newsweek,* July 2, 1973; p. 24.
16. *The New York Times,* January 28, 1976—"5000 at Robeson's Funeral in Harlem" by Charlayne Hunter.
17. *The New York Times,* August 31, 1977—"James [Earl] Jones Gives Robeson Park Lie" by Robert Lindsey.
18. *The New York Times,* March 2, 1978.
19. *Journal,* "Salute to Paul Robeson"; Paul Robeson Archives, Inc., 1973; "Ode to Paul Robeson" by Pablo Neruda, translated by Jill Booty.

Bibliography

Alperovitz, Gar, *Atomic Diplomacy: Hiroshima and Pots-dam.* New York, Simon & Schuster, Inc., 1965; reprint, Vintage Books.

Ambrose, Stephen E., *Rise to Globalism 1938–1970.* Baltimore, Penguin Books, Inc., 1972.

Aptheker, Herbert, ed., *A Documentary History of the Negro People in the U.S.,* 2 vols. New York, Citadel Press, 1964.

Bentley, Eric, ed., *Thirty Years of Treason.* New York, The Viking Press, Inc., 1973.

Bernstein, Barton J., and A. J. Matusow, eds., *The Truman Administration: A Documentary History.* New York, Harper & Row, Publishers, Inc., 1968.

Blaustein, Albert P., and R. L. Zangrando, *Civil Rights and the Black American.* New York, Simon & Schuster, Inc., 1970.

Broderick, Francis, et al., eds., *Black Protest Thought in the Twentieth Century,* 2nd ed. New York, The Bobbs-Merrill Company, Inc., 1971.

Cogley, John, *Report on Blacklisting,* Vols. I and II. The Fund for the Republic, Inc., 1956.

Craven, Avery, W. Johnson, and F. R. Dunn, *A Documentary History of the American People.* Boston, Ginn & Company, 1951.

Davis, Benjamin J., *Communist Councilman from Harlem.* New York, International Publishers Co., Inc., 1969.

Du Bois, W.E.B., *The Autobiography of W.E.B. Du Bois.*
New York, International Publishers Co., Inc., 1969.

Fast, Howard, *Peekskill, USA.* New York, Civil Rights
Congress, 1951.

Feuerlicht, Roberta S., *Joe McCarthy and McCarthyism.*
New York, McGraw-Hill Book Co., 1972.

Freeland, Richard M., *The Truman Doctrine and the Origins of McCarthyism.* New York, Alfred A. Knopf, Inc.,
1972.

Graham, Shirley, *Paul Robeson: Citizen of the World.*
New York, Julian Messner, Inc., 1946.

Hofstadter, Richard M., *The Paranoid Style in American
Politics.* New York, Alfred A. Knopf, Inc., 1965.

Hoyt, Edwin P., *Paul Robeson: The American Othello.*
New York, World Publishing Co., 1967.

Kanfer, Stefan, *A Journal of the Plague Years.* New York,
Atheneum Publishers, 1973.

Kolko, Gabriel, *The Politics of War.* New York, Random
House, Inc., 1968; Vintage Books edition, 1970.

LaFeber, Walter, *America, Russia, and the Cold War,
1945–1971.* New York, John Wiley & Sons, Inc., 1967,
1972.

Morison, Samuel Eliot, H. S. Commager, and W. E. Leuchtenburg, *The Growth of the American Republic,* 2 volumes, 6th ed. New York, Oxford University Press, Inc.,
1969.

Morris, Richard B., *Encyclopedia of American History.*
New York, Harper & Row, Publishers, Inc., 1970.

North, Joseph, ed., *New Masses.* New York, International
Publishers Co., Inc., 1969.

Palmer, R. R., *A History of the Modern World.* New York,
Alfred A. Knopf, Inc., 1969.

Ploski, Harry A., and Roscoe C. Brown, eds., *The Negro
Almanac.* New York, Bellwether Publishing Co., Inc.,
1967.

Robeson, Eslanda Goode, *Paul Robeson, Negro*. New York, Harper & Brothers, 1930.

Robeson, Paul, *Here I Stand*. New York, Othello Associates, 1958; Beacon Press edition, Boston, 1971.

Rubinstein, Annette T. & Associates, eds., *I Vote My Conscience: Vito Marcantonio, Speeches and Writings*. New York, The Vito Marcantonio Memorial, 1956.

Seton, Marie, *Paul Robeson*. London, Dennis Dobson 1958.

Schlesinger, Arthur Meier, *The Rise of Modern America*. New York, The Macmillan Co., 1951.

Schlesinger, Arthur M., Jr., *The Coming of the New Deal*. Boston, Houghton Mifflin Co., 1959.

Stein, Gertrude (Van Vechten, Carl, ed.), *Selected Writings of Gertrude Stein*. New York, Random House, Inc., 1946.

Woollcott, Alexander, *While Rome Burns*. New York, The Viking Press, Inc.

Newspapers and Periodicals
The following publications were used for the periods indicated.

Black World (Negro Digest) March 1950 through November 1970.

The Black Scholar January, February 1970; May, September, 1970.

Christian Century May 1974; September 1949.

Commentary October 1950.

Commonweal September 1949.

Crisis November 1951.

Daily Worker August–September, 1949.

Daily Worker (London) November 1937.

Freedomways 1965, 1969, 1970, 1973.

The Freeman November 1950.

Jet magazine August 1969.

Literary Digest July 1930.

Living Age July 1930; September 1931.

New York *Amsterdam News* 1933–35, 1973.

The Nation May 1950; September 1949.

The New Republic March 1926; August 1930.

Newsweek July–October, 1973.

The New Statesman and Nation August 1936.

The New York Times 1924–1967; 1970–78.

Pittsburgh Courier 1937–1938

Survey March 1925.

Theatre Arts October 1944.

Time magazine 1939–1950; 1970–1973.

Unpublished Sources
Yeakey, Lamont, "Paul Robeson: His Early Nationalist Years." Paper, "Making of a Revolutionary," unpublished thesis. Columbia University, 1971.

Yeakey, Lamont, "Paul Robeson: His Early Nationalist Years." Paper, the Southern Historical Association Meeting, Houston, Texas, 1971.

Schlosser, Anatol I., "Paul Robeson: His Career in the Theatre, in Motion Pictures, and on the Concert Stage," unpublished doctoral dissertation. New York University, 1970.

Acknowledgments

I am indebted to Mark Naison, Institute of Afro-American Studies, Fordham University, for his fine critical reading of and detailed commentary on the manuscript; and to Lamont Yeakey of the Black Economic Research Center, New York, for his constructive criticism.

Appreciation is given to biographer Marie Seten (*Paul Robeson*. Dennis Dobson, London) for pertinent material for which she is the sole source.

I am grateful to Diane Perry, who helped research this book; and to Joe Cali and the staff of the Antioch College Library.

A thanks to special friends—Paul Triechler of the Department of Drama, Antioch College, and the late Jesse Triechler, who opened their files and record collection to me; and acquaintances across the country who freely shared with me their memories of the great Robeson in concert, on the stage and in their homes. Over the years, they held the Robeson experience close to their hearts. They kept the faith.

Ellen Rudin and Elaine Edelman of Harper & Row are responsible for getting me through some difficult stages in the process of publication. Without their faith and confidence in me, this book might not have been written. A special thanks to Ursula Nordstrom, who first worked with me to make an idea a reality.

For my family, who always sustains me, I have the deepest gratitude.

Index